Printed in the United States of America

GEOMETRY PROBLEMS
Review and Workbook
Grades 7-10
555 Questions with Solutions

Published : 08/23/2023

ISBN 13: 9798858038993

Tayyip Oral

GEOMETRY PROBLEMS
Review and Workbook
Grades 7-10

555 Questions with Solutions

Reference Book for

* SAT-ACT
* Include 37 Geometry Topics
* 15 Questions For Every Topic

555 math books series

* 555 Sat Math

* 555 Geometry (555 Questions with Solution)

* 555 Geometry Problems for High School Students

* 555 Act Math (555 Questions with Solution)

* 555 Act Math (555 Questions with Answer)

* 555 Advanced Math Problems – for middle school students

* 555 Math IQ Questions for High School Students

* 555 Math IQ Questions for Middle School Students

* 555 Math IQ Questions for Elementary School Students

* Geometry Formula Handbook.

* Algebra Handbook-for Middle School Students

Table of Contents

TEST SOLUTIONS

PREFACE

Geometry gives you the most effective methods, tips, and strategies for solving geometry problems in both conventional and unconventional ways. The techniques taught in this book allow students to arrive at geometry solutions more quickly and to avoid making careless errors. Perfect in all high school grades students, 555 Geometry teaches lessons, that strengthen geometry skills by focusing on points, lines, rays, angles, triangles, polygons, circles, perimeter, area, and more.

The material in this book includes:

*   555 geometry questions with full solutions
*   37 tests and effective geometry solutions

In addition this book helps students and teachers with ACT and SAT preparations at 300 pages. Readers find a comprehensive review of the most important geometry topics taught in high school specifically.

The practice tests presented in this book are based upon the most recent state level tests and include almost every type of geometry question that one can expect to find on high school level standardized tests.

TEST – 1
(Angles)

1) ∠ACD=70°, ∠BCE=44°, ∠DCE=?

A) 60
B) 62
C) 66
D) 70
E) 76

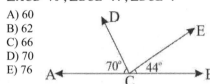

5) BD is the angle bisector of ∠ABC. ∠DBC=44°, ∠ABD=?

A) 44
B) 48
C) 68
D) 70
E) 88

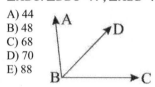

2) x=?

A) 10
B) 15
C) 18
D) 20
E) 22

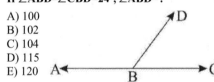

6) ∠ABC is the right angle. ∠DBC=27°, ∠ABD=?

A) 63
B) 64
C) 65
D) 66
E) 73

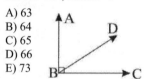

3) If ∠ABD–∠CBD=24°, ∠ABD=?

A) 100
B) 102
C) 104
D) 115
E) 120

7) ∠ABC is the right angle. ∠DBC:∠ABD=1/3, ∠DBC=?

A) 40
B) 30
C) 25
D) 22.5
E) 20

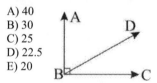

4) BD is the angle bisector of ∠ABC. ∠ABD=34°, ∠ABC=?

A) 34
B) 60
C) 68
D) 70
E) 80

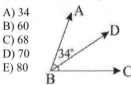

8) BD bisects ∠ABC. Find the value of x.

A) 8
B) 9
C) 10
D) 12
E) 15

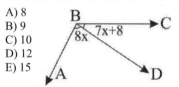

9) BD bisects $\angle ABC$. $\angle ABD=8x-20$, $\angle DBC=3x+30°$
Find the $\angle ABC=?$

A) 100
B) 110
C) 115
D) 120
E) 130

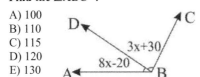

10) $\angle ACF=90°$, $\angle ACE=x$, $\angle ECD=4x$, x=?

A) 10
B) 12
C) 15
D) 18
E) 20

11) $\angle DBC=64°$, $\angle 2x+y=?$

A) 240
B) 244
C) 264
D) 268
E) 270

12) $d_1 \| d_2$ and $d_3 \| d_4$, x=?

A) 36
B) 40
C) 42
D) 44
E) 48

13) $d_1 \| d_2$, x=?

A) 8
B) 10
C) 12
D) 14
E) 16

14) $\angle ABD=82°$, $\angle EBC=4x+2$, 2x=?

A) 30
B) 36
C) 40
D) 80
E) 90

15) $\angle A$ and $\angle B$ are complementary and $\angle A=4x+4$, $\angle B=x+1$. Find the $\angle A$.

A) 42
B) 52
C) 58
D) 62
E) 72

7

TEST – 2
(Angles)

1) $d_1 \| d_2$. Use properties of parallel lines to find the value of x.

A) 10
B) 20
C) 30
D) 40
E) 50

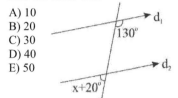

2) $d_1 \| d_2$, x=?

A) 35
B) 40
C) 45
D) 50
E) 55

3) Find the value of the x.

A) 29
B) 30
C) 31
D) 32
E) 39

4) 2x–y=?

A) 80
B) 66
C) 64
D) 44
E) 33

5) $d_1 \| d_2$, y–x=?

A) 30
B) 24
C) 20
D) 18
E) 16

6) $\angle ABC=90°$, $\angle ABD=3x$, $\angle DBC=3y$, x+y=?

A) 90
B) 60
C) 45
D) 30
E) 15

7) x+2y+t=?

A) 180
B) 90
C) 60
D) 45
E) 30

8) $d_1 \| d_2$, x+y=?

A) 114
B) 124
C) 134
D) 144
E) 154

9) $d_1 \| d_2$, x+2y=?

A) 90
B) 100
C) 110
D) 120
E) 130

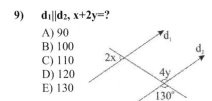

13) $d_1 \| d_2$, 3x+3y=?

A) 30
B) 40
C) 50
D) 60
E) 105

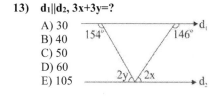

10) $d_1 \| d_2$, x=?

A) 15
B) 20
C) 25
D) 30
E) 40

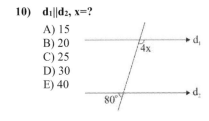

14) x=?

A) 100
B) 105
C) 110
D) 115
E) 120

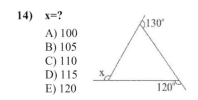

11) $d_1 \| d_2$, x+y=?

A) 106
B) 96
C) 86
D) 76
E) 64

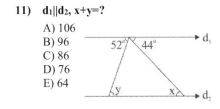

12) x=?

A) 136
B) 126
C) 100
D) 96
E) 86

15) x+y+z=?

A) 100
B) 110
C) 115
D) 120
E) 130

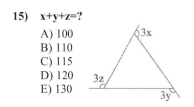

TEST – 3
(Slope – Parallel line – Perpendicular line)

1) Find the slope of the line that passes through the points (0, 8) and (6, 4).

A) $\dfrac{4}{3}$ B) $\dfrac{3}{4}$

C) $\dfrac{2}{3}$ D) 2

E) $-\dfrac{2}{3}$

2) Find the slope of the line that passes through the points (6, 4) and (–4, 8).

A) $-\dfrac{2}{5}$ B) $\dfrac{2}{5}$

C) $\dfrac{5}{2}$ D) $-\dfrac{5}{2}$

E) 2

3) Find the slope of the line that passes through the points $\left(\sqrt{2},\ 2\sqrt{3}\right)$ and $\left(2\sqrt{2},\ \sqrt{27}\right)$.

A) $\sqrt{2}$ B) $\sqrt{3}$

C) $2\sqrt{2}$ D) $2\sqrt{3}$

E) $\dfrac{\sqrt{3}}{\sqrt{2}}$

4) Find the slope of the line that passes through the points (12, 10) and (8, 8).

A) 1   B) $\dfrac{1}{2}$

C) $-\dfrac{1}{2}$ D) –1

E) –2

5) Write and equation of the line through the point (3, 4) that has a slope of 6.

A) y=6x+14   B) y=14x+6

C) y=7x+14   D) y=8x+7

E) y=6x–14

6) Write and equation of the line through the point (8, 9) that has a slope of 3.

A) y=3x–16   B) y=3x–14

C) y=3x–15   D) y=6x–15

E) y=6x–12

7) Line m_1 has the equation y= –2x+6. Line m_2 is parallel to m_1 and passes through the point (2, 6). Write an equation of m_2.

A) y= –2x–6   B) y= –2x–8

C) y=2x+6   D) y= –2x+10

E) y=4x+10

8) Line m_1 has the equation $y = \sqrt{3}x + 6$. Line m_2 is parallel to m_1 and passes through the point $\left(\sqrt{3},\ 2\sqrt{3}\right)$. Write an equation of m_2.

A) $y = \sqrt{3}x + 2\sqrt{3} - 1$

B) $y = \sqrt{3}x - 2\sqrt{3} + 1$

C) $y = \sqrt{3}x + 2\sqrt{3} - 3$

D) $y = \sqrt{3}x + 4\sqrt{3}$

E) $y = -\sqrt{3}x + 2\sqrt{3} - 1$

) y=3x+9. Find the slope of the given equation.

A) –3　　　　B) 3　　　C) 9

D) –9　　　　E) 1

10) 2x+7y+21=0. Find the equation slope.

A) 2　　　　　　　　B) –2

C) $\dfrac{7}{2}$　　　　　　D) $\dfrac{2}{7}$

E) $-\dfrac{2}{7}$

11) $y = \sqrt{3}x + 3\sqrt{3}$. Find the equation slope.

A) $-\sqrt{3}$　　　　　B) $\sqrt{3}$

C) $-3\sqrt{3}$　　　　D) $3\sqrt{3}$

E) $\dfrac{1}{\sqrt{3}}$

12) Line m_1 has equation $y = \dfrac{3x}{2} - \dfrac{7}{3}$.

Find the equation of line m_2 that passes through B(4, –2) and is perpendicular to m_1.

A) $y = \dfrac{2x}{3} + \dfrac{2}{3}$

B) $y = -\dfrac{2x}{3} - \dfrac{2}{3}$

C) $y = -\dfrac{2x}{3} + \dfrac{3}{2}$

D) $y = -\dfrac{2x}{3} + \dfrac{2}{3}$

E) $y = \dfrac{2x}{3} + \dfrac{14}{3}$

13) m_1 equation line: y=7x+4;
m_2 equation line: y=ax+12;
m_1 is perpendicular of m_2 line. Find the a?

A) 7　　　　　　　　　　B) –7

C) $\dfrac{1}{7}$　　　　　　　　D) $-\dfrac{1}{4}$

E) $-\dfrac{1}{7}$

14) Find an equation of the line. Slope=4, y–intercept=6.

A) y=4x+6　　　　　B) y= –4x+6

C) y=6x+6　　　　　D) y=6x+4

E) y= –4x–6

15) m_1 line: $y = \dfrac{2x}{3} + 7$. m_2 line:

$y = \dfrac{3x}{5} + 4$. Find the sum of slopes.

A) $\dfrac{15}{19}$　　　　　　B) $-\dfrac{15}{19}$

C) $\dfrac{19}{15}$　　　　　　D) $-\dfrac{19}{15}$

E) 3

TEST – 4
(Slope)

1) $y=4x+12$, find the slope.

A) –4   B) 4

C) 12   D) $\dfrac{1}{3}$

E) –3

2) $3x+6y+18=0$, find the slope of the line

A) 3   B) –3
C) 6   D) –6

E) $-\dfrac{1}{2}$

3) $y = \sqrt{3}x + 3\sqrt{3}$, find the equation slope.

A) $\sqrt{3}$ B) $-\sqrt{3}$

C) $3\sqrt{3}$ D) $-3\sqrt{3}$

E) $-\dfrac{1}{\sqrt{3}}$

4) $\sqrt{2}x + \sqrt{3}y + 6 = 0$, find the equation slope.

A) $\dfrac{\sqrt{2}}{\sqrt{3}}$ B) $\dfrac{\sqrt{3}}{\sqrt{2}}$

C) $\dfrac{-\sqrt{2}}{\sqrt{3}}$ D) $-\sqrt{2}$

E) $\sqrt{3}$

5) Line m has equation $y=4x+12$, which equation can be parallel to m line?

A) $y=-4x+12$ B) $y=3x+10$
C) $y=12x+4$ D) $y=-12x+6$
E) $y=4x+4$

6) m_1 line: $2x+3y+6=0$; m_2 line: $ax+4y+12=0$; $m_1\|m_2$ if a=?

A) 3   B) 8

C) $\dfrac{3}{8}$ D) $\dfrac{8}{3}$

E) 6

7) m_1 line: $7x+6y=14$;
m_2 line: $ax+4y=12$;
m_1 line is perpendicular m_2, find the a=?

A) $-\dfrac{14}{3}$ B) $\dfrac{14}{3}$

C) $\dfrac{3}{14}$ D) $\dfrac{3}{10}$

E) $-\dfrac{24}{7}$

8) Find the d_1 line equation.

A) $\dfrac{x}{4}+\dfrac{y}{2}=1$

B) $\dfrac{x}{2}+\dfrac{y}{4}=-1$

C) $\dfrac{x}{2}+\dfrac{y}{4}=1$

D) $\dfrac{x}{2}+\dfrac{y}{4}=4$

E) $2x+4y=4$

9) **Find the d₁ line equation.**

A) $\dfrac{x}{7} - \dfrac{y}{7} = 1$

B) $\dfrac{x}{7} + \dfrac{y}{7} = 14$

C) 7x+7y=14

D) x+y=14

E) x+y=7

10) **A(3, 4), B(9, 13), find the slope of $\overrightarrow{AB}$?**

A) $\dfrac{1}{3}$

B) $\dfrac{1}{2}$

C) $\dfrac{3}{4}$

D) $\dfrac{4}{3}$

E) $\dfrac{3}{2}$

11) **A$\left(\sqrt{5}, 2\sqrt{3}\right)$, B$\left(\sqrt{20}, \sqrt{75}\right)$, find the slope of $\overrightarrow{AB}$?**

A) $\dfrac{\sqrt{3}}{\sqrt{5}}$

B) $\dfrac{\sqrt{5}}{\sqrt{3}}$

C) $\dfrac{2\sqrt{5}}{3}$

D) $\dfrac{3}{\sqrt{5}}$

E) $\dfrac{3\sqrt{3}}{5}$

12) **A$\left(\dfrac{1}{4}, \dfrac{1}{6}\right)$, B$\left(\dfrac{1}{2}, \dfrac{1}{3}\right)$, find the slope of $\overline{AB}$?**

A) 1

B) 2

C) –2

D) $\dfrac{3}{2}$

E) $\dfrac{1}{3}$

13) $\dfrac{2x}{3} + \dfrac{3y}{2} + 6 = 0$, **find the slope?**

A) $-\dfrac{4}{9}$

B) $\dfrac{4}{9}$

C) $\dfrac{9}{4}$

D) $-\dfrac{9}{4}$

E) 2

14) **Find the d₁ line equation.**

A) x+y=6

B) x+y=–6

C) y=x–6

D) y=–x+12

E) 2x+y=6

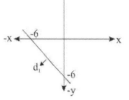

15) **Find the d₁ line equation.**

A) $\dfrac{x}{4} + \dfrac{y}{6} = 1$

B) $\dfrac{x}{6} + \dfrac{y}{4} = 1$

C) $\dfrac{x}{4} - \dfrac{y}{6} = 1$

D) $\dfrac{x}{4} - \dfrac{y}{6} = -1$

E) 4x+6y=24

TEST – 5
(Triangles and Angles)

1) AB=AC, ∠A=54°, ∠B=?

   A) 62
   B) 63
   C) 64
   D) 65
   E) 66

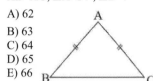

5) ∠B=90°, ∠A=∠C=2x,
   Find the value of 4x.

   A) 60
   B) 70
   C) 80
   D) 84
   E) 90

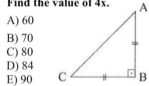

2) ∠A=60°, ∠ACD=110°,
   ∠B=x=?

   A) 40
   B) 44
   C) 50
   D) 54
   E) 60

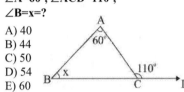

6) ∠A=122°, AB=AC, ∠B=?

   A) 30
   B) 29
   C) 28
   D) 27
   E) 26

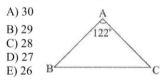

3) ∠A=48°, ∠B=90°, ∠ACD=3x, x=?

   A) 40
   B) 42
   C) 44
   D) 46
   E) 50

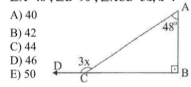

7) ∠A=70°, ∠B=60°, ∠C=50°.

   A) AB>BC>AC
   B) BC>AC>AB
   C) AC>AB>BC
   D) BA>BC>AC
   E) AB=AC>BC

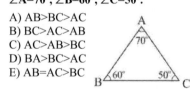

4) ∠A=3x, ∠C=2x, ∠B=90°, 4x=?

   A) 60
   B) 54
   C) 70
   D) 72
   E) 80

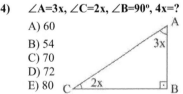

8) x=?

   A) 108
   B) 109
   C) 110
   D) 120
   E) 121

9) 2x+3y=?

A) 260

B) 270
C) 280
D) 290
E) 300

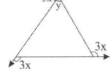

10) α=?

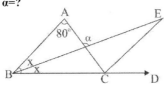

A) x   B) 2x
C) 80+2x   D) x+80
E) 80–x

11) BD=DC=AD, ∠C=2x,
∠B=y, y+2x=?

A) 60

B) 70
C) 80
D) 90
E) 100

12) AB=AC, AD=DC, x=?

A) 90–3α
B) 90–2α
C) 180–3α
D) 180–4α
E) 90+2α

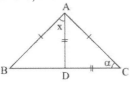

13) ∠ADC=90º, ∠C=90º,
∠DAC=64º, ∠E=α=?

A) 24
B) 26
C) 28
D) 30
E) 32

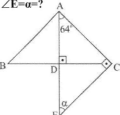

14) AB=AC, BD=BC, 3a=?

A) 90+m
B) 90–m
C) 180+m
D) 180+2m
E) 540-3x

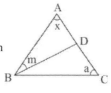

15) AB=BC=AC, AC=DC,
∠D=2x, x²=?

A) 144
B) 225
C) 169
D) 289
E) 900

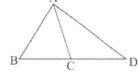

TEST – 6
(Congruence and Triangles)

* ∠A=23°, ∠F=(4y–5)°,
ΔABC ≅ FED

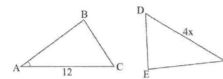

1) **Find the value of x?**

   A) 1   B) 2
   C) 3   D) 4
   E) 5

2) **Find the value of y?**

   A) 8   B) 7
   C) 6   D) 5
   E) 4

* AE=12, ∠D=42°, FL=4x+4,
∠K=(5y–8)°,   ABCDE ≅ FGHKL

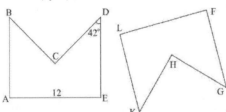

3) **Find the value of x?**

   A) 6   B) 5
   C) 4   D) 3
   E) 2

4) **Find the value of y?**

   A) 15   B) 14
   C) 12   D) 11
   E) 10

5) ∠A=∠E, x=?

   A) 66
   B) 64
   C) 60
   D) 50
   E) 33

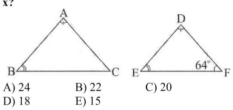

6) ∠F=64°, ∠C=(3x+4)°, Find the value of
x?

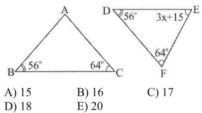

   A) 24   B) 22   C) 20
   D) 18   E) 15

7) ∠B=∠D=56°, ∠E=(3x+15),
∠C=∠F=64°, Find the value of x?

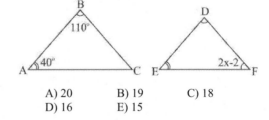

   A) 15   B) 16   C) 17
   D) 18   E) 20

8) ∠ABC ≅ EDF, ∠B=110°, ∠A=40°,
∠F=2x–2. Find the value of x?

   A) 20   B) 19   C) 18
   D) 16   E) 15

9) Given ∠A=∠E, and ∠D=∠B, ∠C=2m+6, Find the value of m?

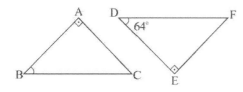

A) 15   B) 14   C) 10
D) 9   E) 8

10) Given △ABC ≅ △DEF, ∠A=50°, ∠C=65°, ∠E=(4m+5)°, Find the value of 2m?

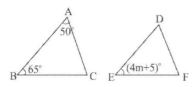

A) 30   B) 32   C) 40
D) 42   E) 60

11) DE∥BA, x=?

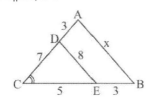

A) $\dfrac{60}{7}$ B) $\dfrac{70}{8}$ C) $\dfrac{80}{7}$

D) $\dfrac{60}{17}$ E) $\dfrac{70}{9}$

12) DE∥BC, AE=4, EC=3, DE=6, x=?

A) $\dfrac{21}{2}$

B) $\dfrac{21}{4}$

C) $\dfrac{22}{3}$

D) $\dfrac{22}{5}$

E) 7

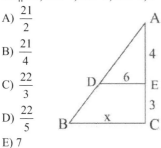

13) AB∥DE, DE=m=?

A) 30
B) 28
C) 26
D) 24
E) 22

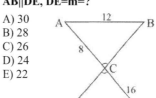

14) ∠B=∠D=90°, AB=4, ABC ≅ EDC, BC=8, DC=16, DE=m=?

A) 7
B) 8
C) 9
D) 10
E) 11

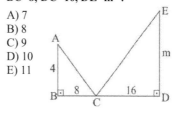

15) CDE ≅ CAB, x=?

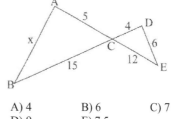

A) 4   B) 6   C) 7
D) 9   E) 7,5

TEST – 7
(Isosceles, Equilateral Right Triangle)

1) AB=AC, ∠A=80°, ∠B=?

A) 60
B) 50
C) 48
D) 44
E) 42

2) AB=AC, ∠A=2x, ∠B=x, ∠C=?

A) 45
B) 44
C) 43
D) 42
E) 40

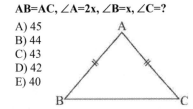

3) AB=AC, ∠ACD=134°, ∠A=?

A) 90
B) 89
C) 88
D) 87
E) 86

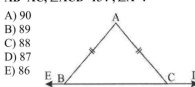

4) AB=AC, ∠A=x, ∠B=2y, x=?

A) x=180+2y
B) x=180–2y
C) x=90–2y
D) x=180+4y
E) x=180–4y

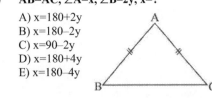

5) AB=AC, AB=24, AC=4x+4, x=?

A) 8
B) 7
C) 6
D) 5
E) 4

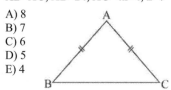

6) AB=AC, ∠A=88°, ∠A–∠C=?

A) 52
B) 42
C) 32
D) 22
E) 12

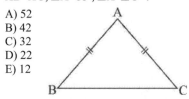

7) AB=AC, ABC is isosceles triangle, DEF is the equilateral triangle. Find the difference perimeter P(DEF) – P(ABC) =?

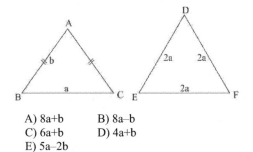

A) 8a+b   B) 8a–b
C) 6a+b   D) 4a+b
E) 5a–2b

8) ABC is the isosceles triangle, ∠A=86°, DEF is the equilateral triangle. (∠F):(∠B)=?

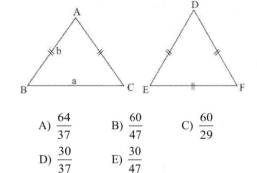

A) $\frac{64}{37}$ B) $\frac{60}{47}$ C) $\frac{60}{29}$

D) $\frac{30}{37}$ E) $\frac{30}{47}$

9) ABC is the equilateral triangle. y−x=?

A) 60
B) 50
C) 40
D) 30
E) 20

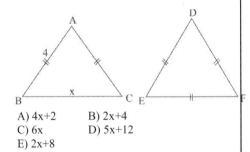

10) ABC is the isosceles triangle, AB=4, BC=x, DEF is the equilateral triangle, DF=x+4. Find the difference perimeter P(DEF) − P(ABC) =?

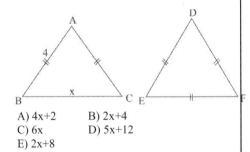

A) 4x+2   B) 2x+4
C) 6x   D) 5x+12
E) 2x+8

11) ABC is the isosceles triangle, ∠A=x, ∠B=x+20°, x=?

A) $\dfrac{130}{3}$

B) $\dfrac{130}{7}$

C) $\dfrac{140}{5}$

D) $\dfrac{140}{3}$

E) $\dfrac{170}{4}$

12) Find the sum all triangle perimeters.

A) 70
B) 64
C) 60
D) 50
E) 52

13) ABC, DCE, FEK, are the equilateral triangles. BK=12cm, Find the sum all triangle perimeters.

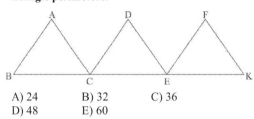

A) 24   B) 32   C) 36
D) 48   E) 60

14) ABC is the right triangle and AB=BC, DEF is the equilateral triangle. ∠F−∠C=?

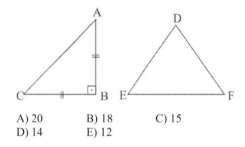

A) 20   B) 18   C) 15
D) 14   E) 12

15) ACD is the equilateral triangle. ∠BAC=20°, ∠B=2x, x=?

A) 15
B) 18
C) 19
D) 20
E) 24

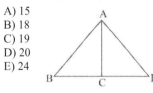

TEST – 8

(Bisectors, median of a triangle)

1) If ∠ABD is bisected by ray $\overrightarrow{BD}$. ∠B=90°. What is the value of x?

A) $\dfrac{20}{3}$

B) $\dfrac{40}{3}$

C) $\dfrac{40}{7}$

D) $\dfrac{80}{7}$

E) $\dfrac{80}{3}$

2) If ∠ABF and ∠CBD are bisected by FB and BD. What is the (m+n)?

A) 90
B) 80
C) 70
D) 60
E) 50

*   ∠AEB=60°, ∠A=90°, BE and FC are bisectors.

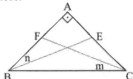

3) Find the (m+n)=?

A) 30   B) 36   C) 40   D) 45 E) 60

4) Find the ∠n–∠m=?

A) 15   B) 20   C) 25   D) 30 E) 45

5) ABC is the triangle. What is the length of $\overrightarrow{DC}$?

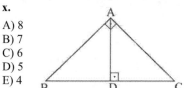

A) $\dfrac{7}{20}$

B) $\dfrac{30}{7}$

C) $\dfrac{7}{30}$

D) $\dfrac{40}{7}$

E) 5

6) AD is the perpendicular bisector of BC. BD=6x–9, DC=2x+11, Find the value of x.

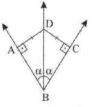

A) 8
B) 7
C) 6
D) 5
E) 4

7) ∠ABD=7x+10°, ∠DBC=4x+40, x=?

A) 7
B) 8
C) 9
D) 10
E) 12

8) ∠ABC=124°, BD is the bisector. Find the ∠DBC=?

A) 50
B) 54
C) 58
D) 60
E) 62

9) $\overline{AD}$ and $\overline{BE}$ are median. AE=4, BD=5, Find the ration (DC):(CE)

A) $\dfrac{4}{5}$

B) $\dfrac{5}{4}$

C) $\dfrac{6}{5}$

D) $\dfrac{5}{6}$

E) $\dfrac{10}{9}$

10) $\overline{AD}$ and $\overline{BE}$ are the median. AD=27 and BE=30, Find the ratio (BK):(AK).

A) $\dfrac{8}{9}$

B) $\dfrac{7}{9}$

C) $\dfrac{8}{7}$

D) 4

E) $\dfrac{9}{10}$

11) K is the centroid of ABC and KF=8cm. Find the KB=?

A) 10
B) 12
C) 14
D) 15
E) 16

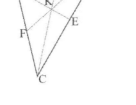

12) D is the centroid of ABC. If AF=72cm find the DF?

A) 10
B) 12
C) 16
D) 18

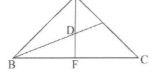

E) 24

13) E is the centroid of ABC. $\overline{AD}$ and $\overline{BF}$ are median. $DE = 2\sqrt{3}$, Find the AD=?

A) $2\sqrt{3}$

B) $3\sqrt{3}$

C) $4\sqrt{3}$

D) $5\sqrt{3}$

E) $6\sqrt{3}$

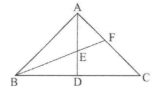

14) AD is the bisector of △ABC. Find the x=?

A) 5
B) 6
C) 7
D) 6.6
E) 7.2

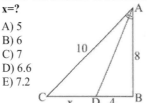

15) AD is the bisector of △ABC. $AB = 5\sqrt{3}$, $AC = 6\sqrt{3}$, $BD = 3\sqrt{3}$, DC=?

A) $\dfrac{6\sqrt{3}}{5}$

B) $\dfrac{7\sqrt{3}}{5}$

C) $4\sqrt{3}$

D) $5\sqrt{3}$

E) $\dfrac{18\sqrt{3}}{5}$

TEST – 9
(Polygons)

1) **Find the ∠B=?**

A) 80
B) 75
C) 70
D) 65
E) 60

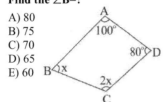

5) ∠A=90°, ∠B=88°, ∠C=2x, ∠D=94°, x=?

A) 40
B) 42
C) 43
D) 44
E) 50

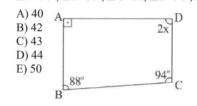

2) ∠x=?

A) 101
B) 91
C) 81
D) 71
E) 61

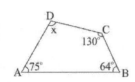

6) ∠A+∠D=?

A) 180
B) 170
C) 160
D) 150
E) 140

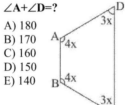

3) ∠A=?

A) 82
B) 72
C) 62
D) 52
E) 42

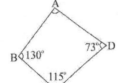

7) ∠D=120°, ∠A=54°, ∠B=64, ∠C=?

A) 120
B) 122
C) 132
D) 136
E) 140

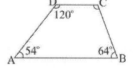

4) x=?

A) 26
B) 27
C) 28
D) 29
E) 30

8) x=?

A) 10
B) 15
C) 18
D) 20
E) 22

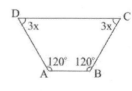

9) ∠A=5x°, ∠B=80°, ∠C=64°, ∠D=7x°, ∠A=?

A) 90
B) 85
C) 80
D) 70
E) 65

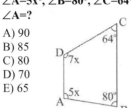

10) AB=BC=DC=ED=EF=FA, ∠A+∠E=?

A) 100
B) 110
C) 120
D) 140
E) 240

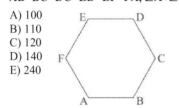

11) ∠A=78°, ∠B=61°, ∠C=79°, x=?

A) 144
B) 142
C) 141
D) 130
E) 131

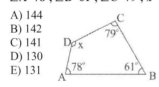

12) ∠A=∠B=74°, ∠C=∠D=2x, x=?

A) 64
B) 60
C) 57
D) 53
E) 52

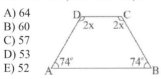

13) ∠D=90°, ∠A=88°, ∠B=64°, ∠C=?

A) 118
B) 120
C) 121
D) 124
E) 130

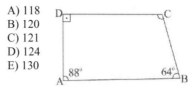

14) Find the x=?

A) 140
B) 148
C) 150
D) 151
E) 161

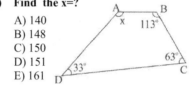

15) ∠B=110°, ∠C=120°, ∠D=20°, ∠A=x =?

A) 110
B) 115
C) 120
D) 130
E) 140

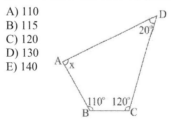

TEST – 10
(Midsegment theorem, midpoint formula)

1) EF||BC, BC=26cm, EF=?

A) 12
B) 13
C) 14
D) 15
E) 16

2) DE||BC, DE=19cm, BC=?

A) 36
B) 37
C) 38
D) 39
E) 40

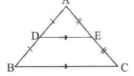

3) DE||BC, DE=3x, BC=4x+6, BC+DE=?

A) 27
B) 28
C) 30
D) 34
E) 36

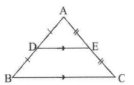

4) DE||BC, DE=x+6, BC=3x+4, x=?

A) 8
B) 6
C) 5
D) 4
E) 2

5) KE=14, KD=11, AC+BC=?

A) 50
B) 52
C) 54
D) 58
E) 60

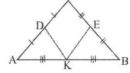

6) DE=4x+6y, BC =?

A) 2x+3y
B) 2x+6y
C) 8x+6y
D) 8x+12y
E) 8x+11y

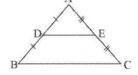

7) DE=2^{12}, BC=?

A) 2^6
B) 2^8
C) 2^9
D) 2^{10}
E) 2^{13}

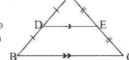

8) FD=2^x, FE=3^x, AC+BA=?

A) $\dfrac{2^x+3^x}{3}$

B) $\dfrac{2^x+3^x}{2}$

C) $\dfrac{6^x}{2}$

D) $\dfrac{2^x+3^x}{4}$

E) $2\cdot(2^x+3^x)$

9) Point A is at (–8, –10) and point B is at (–6, 14). What is the midpoint of line segment AB?

    A) (–7, –2)
    B) (–7, 2)
    C) (–8, –4)
    D) (–2, 7)
    E) (–7, –6)

10) A(–6, 10), B(4, 8). Find the midpoint of line segment $\overrightarrow{AB}$.

    A) (–1, –9)   B) (–2, 9)
    C) (9, –1)   D) (–1, 9)
    E) (–2, 8)

11) K is the midpoint of AB. The coordinated K(–2, 3) and A(4, 2) are given. Find the coordinates of point B.

    A) (–8, 8)   B) (6, –8)
    C) (10, 4)   D) (–8, 4)
    E) (–7, –6)

12) What is the midpoint of the straight line segment joining the points (–4, 8) and (–6, 12)?

    A) (–5, –8)   B) (–5, 10)
    C) (10, –5)   D) (5, 10)
    E) (–6, 10)

13) A (–2, 6), B(6, 7), C(8, –3). What is the midpoint of AB?

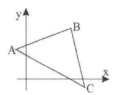

    A) $\left(1, \dfrac{7}{2}\right)$ B) $\left(2, \dfrac{7}{3}\right)$

    C) $\left(2, 6\dfrac{1}{2}\right)$ D) $\left(3, 6\dfrac{1}{2}\right)$

    E) $\left(6\dfrac{1}{2}, 2\right)$

14) A(–8, 6), B(–3, –10) and C(5, –2). What is the midpoint of BC?

    A) (–1, –6)
    B) (–1, –7)
    C) (1, –6)
    D) (–6, 1)
    E) (2, –3)

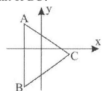

15) A(–12, 10), B(20, –6), AC=CD=DE=EB, What are the coordinates of E?

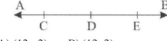

    A) (12, -2)   B) (12, 2)
    C) (-2, 12)   D) (6, 12)
    E) (8, 4)

TEST – 11
(Parallelograms)

1) $\angle A=68^{o}$, $\angle B–\angle C=?$

A) 44
B) 46
C) 48
D) 50
E) 54

5) ABCD is parallelogram.
$\angle C=66^{o}$, $\angle A=3m$, $\angle B=2n$, $n+m=?$

A) 30
B) 40
C) 50
D) 60
E) 80

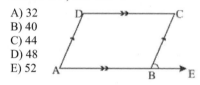

2) ABCD is parallelogram.
$\angle B=124^{o}$, $\angle A=2x$, $x=?$

A) 40
B) 30
C) 28
D) 14
E) 13

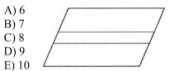

6) ABCD is parallelogram.
$\angle CBE=64^{o}$, $\angle D–\angle A=?$

A) 32
B) 40
C) 44
D) 48
E) 52

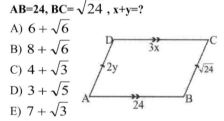

3) How many parallelogram in the figure?

A) 6
B) 7
C) 8
D) 9
E) 10

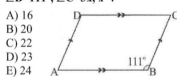

7) ABCD is parallelogram.
$AB=24$, $BC=\sqrt{24}$, $x+y=?$

A) $6+\sqrt{6}$
B) $8+\sqrt{6}$
C) $4+\sqrt{3}$
D) $3+\sqrt{5}$
E) $7+\sqrt{3}$

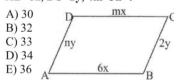

4) ABCD is parallelogram.
$\angle B=111^{o}$, $\angle C=3x$, $x=?$

A) 16
B) 20
C) 22
D) 23
E) 24

8) ABCD is parallelogram.
$AB=6x$, $BC=2y$, $4m+3n=?$

A) 30
B) 32
C) 33
D) 34
E) 36

9) $x=?$

A) 65
B) 64
C) 55
D) 54
E) 53

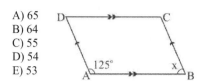

the parallelogram's perimeters.

A) 64
B) 74
C) 84
D) 90
E) 98

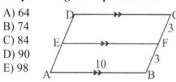

10) **ABCD is the parallelogram.** $\angle A=8n$, $\angle B=4m$, $2n+m=?$

A) 120
B) 60
C) 55
D) 45
E) 30

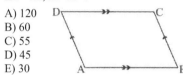

14) **ABCD is the parallelogram.**
$DE=\sqrt{12}$, $EC=\sqrt{24}$, $AC+BD=?$

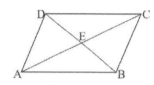

11) **Find the perimeter of ABCD.**

A) 28
B) 29
C) 30
D) 34
E) 48

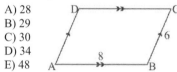

A) $3\sqrt{3}+3\sqrt{6}$ B) $4\sqrt{3}+4\sqrt{2}$
C) $4\sqrt{3}+4\sqrt{6}$ D) $4\sqrt{6}+5\sqrt{3}$
E) $4\sqrt{6}+3\sqrt{5}$

12) **ABCD is the parallelogram.** $AB=2^8$cm, $BC=2^6$cm, $P(ABCD)=2^A \cdot B$. if B is odd find $A+B=?$

A) 10
B) 11
C) 12
D) 13
E) 14

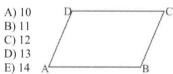

13) **AB=10, BF=FC=3, Find the sum all**

15) **$AE=9^x$, $BE=3^x$, $(AC) \cdot (BD)=m \cdot 3^{nx}$, $m+n=?$**

A) 9
B) 8
C) 7
D) 6
E) 5

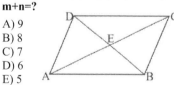

TEST – 12
(Rhombuses, Rectangles and Squares)

1) ABCD is the rhombuses.
AB=3y, BC=2y+6, DC=?

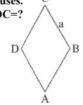

A) 20
B) 18
C) 16
D) 15
E) 14

2) ABCD is the square.
AL=LB=BE=EC.
How many square
in the figure?

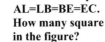

A) 5
B) 6
C) 7
D) 8
E) 10

3) ABCD is the square.
∠BAC=3x, ∠ABC=3y,
y–x=?

A) 20
B) 18
C) 17
D) 16
E) 15

4) ABCD is the rhomb.
∠A=64°, ∠C=2x, x=?

A) 23
B) 24
C) 30
D) 40
E) 32

5) ABCD is the parallelogram.
$AC=\sqrt{54}$, $BD=\sqrt{24}$,
2AE–BE=?

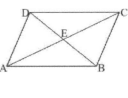

A) $\sqrt{6}$
B) $2\sqrt{6}$
C) $2\sqrt{3}$
D) $\dfrac{2\sqrt{3}}{3}$
E) $\dfrac{\sqrt{6}}{2}$

6) ABCD is the rectangle. AB=3x+6,
DC=30, AD=25, BC=5y+5, 2x+y=?

A) 30
B) 28
C) 26
D) 25
E) 20

7) ABCD is the rectangle. KLMN is
the square. AB=8, BC=6, $KL=\sqrt{28}$,
P(KLMN):P(ABCD)=?

A) $\dfrac{\sqrt{14}}{2}$ B) $\dfrac{3\sqrt{7}}{2}$

C) $\dfrac{1}{\sqrt{7}}$ D) $\dfrac{2}{\sqrt{7}}$

E) 2

8) ABCD is the rhomb. KLMN is the square. BC=3^xcm, KL=9^x, P(KLMN):P(ABCD)=?

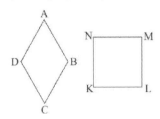

A) 1   B) 2

C) $\dfrac{1}{3^x}$ D) 3^x

E) 3^{2x}

9) ABCD is rectangle. KLMN is square. P(ABCD)+P(KLMN)=32cm, 3a+b=?

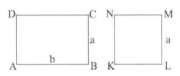

A) 32   B) 20   C) 18
D) 16   E) 14

10) ABCD is the square. AB=4^x, KLMN is the rhomb. KL=4, P(ABCD):P(KLMN)=?

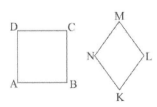

A) 4^x B) 4^{x+1} C) 4^{x-1}
D) 4^{2x} E) 1

11) ABCD is the square. AE=4cm, BD=?

A) 6
B) 7
C) 8
D) 9
E) 10

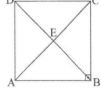

12) ABCD is the rhomb. AC=18, BD=24, BE+EC=?

A) 25
B) 24
C) 23
D) 22
E) 21

13) ABCD is the square.

AC=$2\sqrt{6}$ cm, P(ABCD)=?

A) $4\sqrt{3}$
B) $6\sqrt{3}$
C) $8\sqrt{3}$
D) $12\sqrt{3}$
E) $16\sqrt{3}$

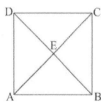

14) ABCD is the rectangle. AB=2, BC=1, $\dfrac{P(ABCD)}{(AC+BD)}=?$

A) $\dfrac{6}{5}$ B) $\dfrac{6}{\sqrt{5}}$ C) $\dfrac{6}{2\sqrt{5}}$

D) $\dfrac{7}{\sqrt{5}}$ E) $\dfrac{8}{\sqrt{5}}$

15) **ABCD is the rectangle. AB=16, BC=12, |AE|:|BC|=?**

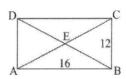

A) $\dfrac{10}{13}$ B) $\dfrac{5}{6}$ C) $\dfrac{6}{5}$

D) $\dfrac{13}{10}$ E) 2

TEST – 13
(Trapezoid)

1) ABCD is an isosceles trapezoid.
∠A=48°. Find the ∠B.

A) 124
B) 128
C) 130
D) 132
E) 48

2) EF is the midsegment.
DC=8cm, AB=14cm, EF=?

A) 10
B) 11
C) 12
D) 13
E) 14

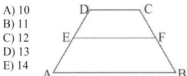

3) ∠D=46°. ∠B=?

A) 114
B) 124
C) 134
D) 144
E) 148

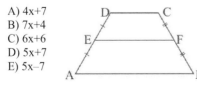

4) EF is the midsegment.
DC=2x+4, AB=6x+10, EF=?

A) 4x+7
B) 7x+4
C) 6x+6
D) 5x+7
E) 5x–7

5) EF is the midsegment.
BC=6, EF=14, AD=?

A) 18
B) 19
C) 20
D) 21
E) 22

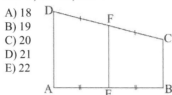

6) AB=6x+2, DC=2x+6, EF=12, x=?

A) 2
B) 3
C) 4
D) 5
E) 6

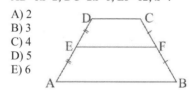

7) ∠B=130°, ∠D=40°, ∠A=?

A) 65
B) 75
C) 85
D) 95
E) 98

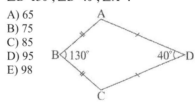

8) ∠A=80°, ∠B=112°,
∠C=?

A) 50
B) 52
C) 56
D) 58
E) 60

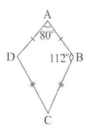

9) ABCD is the trapezoid. DE=4, EA=6, AB=12, DC=8, x=?

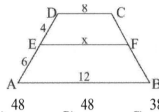

A) $\dfrac{48}{7}$ B) $\dfrac{48}{5}$ C) $\dfrac{38}{7}$

D) $\dfrac{38}{5}$ E) 6

0) ABCD is the trapezoid. DC∥AB, DE∥BC, x=?

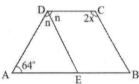

A) 81   B) 84   C) 71   D) 61   E) 51

11) ABCD is the trapezoid. EF is the midsegment. If $\dfrac{DC}{AB}=\dfrac{1}{7}$, find

$$\frac{EF}{AB+DC}=?$$

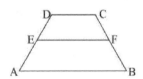

A) $\dfrac{5}{11}$ B) $\dfrac{4}{11}$ C) $\dfrac{1}{2}$

D) $\dfrac{11}{7}$ E) $\dfrac{13}{6}$

12) ABCD is the trapezoid. AD=BC, α=?

A) 36
B) 37
C) 38
D) 39
E) 40

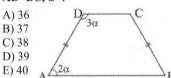

13) ABCD is the trapezoid. EF is the midsegment. AB=mx, DC=nx, EF=?

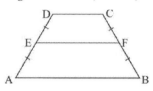

A) mx–nx   B) mx+nx

C) $\dfrac{mx+nx}{2}$ D) 2mx+nx

E) 2mx – nx

14) ABCD is the trapezoid. EF is the midsegment, AB=2^{2x+2}, DC=2^{x+1}, EF=?

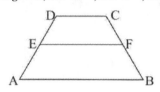

A) $2^{2x+1}+2^{x}$ B) 2^{2x+1}
C) $2^{2x}+2^{x}$ D) $2^{2x}+2^{3x}$
E) $2^{3x}+2^{1}$

15) ABCD is the trapezoid. AD=16cm, BC=10cm, EF=22cm, Find the perimeter ABCD?

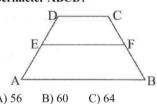

A) 56   B) 60   C) 64
D) 68   E) 70

TEST – 14
(Areas of triangles and Quadrilaterals)

1) ABC is the triangle. AB=12, DC=4,
Find the area of △ABC.

A) 48
B) 36
C) 24
D) 20
E) 18

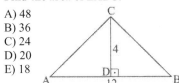

2) ABC is the triangle. AB=14, BC=6, Find
the area of △ABC.

A) 42
B) 44
C) 46
D) 48
E) 50

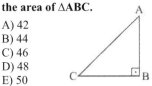

3) AB=x+4, BC=6,
A(ABC)=24cm², x=?

A) 2
B) 3
C) 4
D) 5
E) 6

4) A(ABC)=36, CB=12, DA=?

A) 3
B) 4
C) 5
D) 6
E) 7

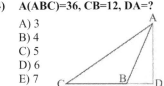

5) A(ABC)=24sq unit.
AB+BC=?

A) 9
B) 10
C) 11
D) 12
E) 14

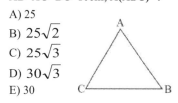

6) AB=AC=BC=10cm, A(ABC)=?

A) 25
B) $25\sqrt{2}$
C) $25\sqrt{3}$
D) $30\sqrt{3}$
E) 30

7) ABC is the triangle. ∠A=∠C=45º,
A(ABC)=12cm², BC=?

A) $2\sqrt{2}$
B) $2\sqrt{3}$
C) $2\sqrt{5}$
D) $2\sqrt{6}$
E) $3\sqrt{6}$

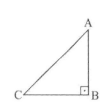

8) ∠B=α=30º, AB=6,
BC=8, A(ABC)=?

A) 12
B) 16
C) 24
D) 28
E) 48

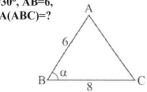

9) ABC is the triangle. BD=DE=EC,

A(ABD)=6cm², A(ABC)=?

A) 12
B) 16
C) 18
D) 24
E) 36

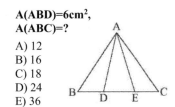

13) A(ADE)=7cm², A(ABC)=?

A) 14
B) 18
C) 24
D) 28
E) 36

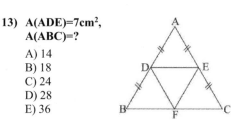

10) $\dfrac{BD}{DC} = \dfrac{3}{5}$, A(ABD)=15cm², A(ABC)=?

A) 40
B) 38
C) 35
D) 30
E) 25

14) ABC is the triangle. A(ABC)=100cm², $\dfrac{CD}{DB} = \dfrac{3}{7}$, if A(ACD)=?

A) 30
B) 35
C) 40
D) 45
E) 48

11) ABC is the triangle. AB=8, A(ADC)=24, DC=?

A) 10
B) 9
C) 8
D) 7
E) 6

15) $BD = \sqrt{6}$, $DC = \sqrt{12}$, A(ABD):A(ADC)=?

A) 1   B) 2   C) $\sqrt{2}$

D) $\dfrac{1}{\sqrt{2}}$ E) $\dfrac{1}{3}$

12) ABC is the triangle. AC=16, BD=6, BC=10, AE=?

A) 6.6
B) 7.6
C) 8.6
D) 9.6
E) 10.6

TEST – 15
(Area of the Square)

1) ABCD is the square. AC=20cm. Find the area of the □ABCD.

A) 50
B) 80
C) 100
D) 150
E) 200

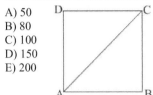

2) ABCD is the square. Perimeter ABCD is 44cm. Find the area of the □ABCD.

A) 11
B) 22
C) 44
D) 88
E) 121

3) ABCD is the square. Perimeter ABCD is 4π. Find the area of the □ABCD.

A) π
B) 2π
C) π²
D) 4π²
E) 4π

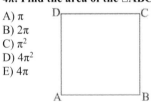

4) ABCD is the square. AB=7ˣcm. Find the area of the □ABCD.

A) 7^{3x}
B) 7^{2x}
C) $4 \cdot 7^x$
D) $8 \cdot 7^x$
E) 49^{2x}

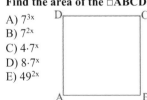

5) ABCD is the square. AB=3π. A(ABCD):P(ABCD)=?

A) 3π
B) 4π
C) $\dfrac{3\pi}{4}$
D) $\dfrac{4\pi}{3}$
E) 6π

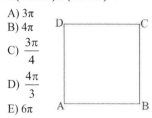

6) ABCD is the square. AE=4cm. Find the area of the □ABCD.

A) 30
B) 32
C) 36
D) 48
E) 64

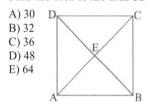

7) ABCD is the square. A(BEC)=22cm². Find the area of ΔDAB.

A) 44
B) 40
C) 36
D) 32
E) 30

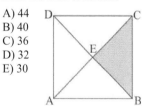

8) ABCD is the square. AB=2ˣcm. Find the ratio Perimeter (ABCD):Area(ABCD).

A) 2^x B) 2^{-x}

C) $4 \cdot 2^x$ D) $\dfrac{4}{2^x}$

E) $\dfrac{1}{2^{4x}}$

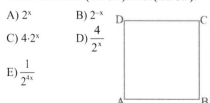

9) ABCD is the square. △(ABE)=50cm². Find the perimeter □ABCD.

A) 20
B) 40
C) 42
D) 44
E) 48

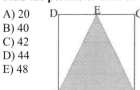

10) ABCD is the square. A(BEC)=36cm². Find the perimeter □ABCD.

A) 48   B) 50
C) 52   D) 54
E) 60

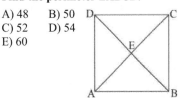

11) ABCD is the square. AL=LB=BK=KC. AD=4cm. Find the sum of all square's areas.

A) 32   B) 34
C) 36   D) 40
E) 44

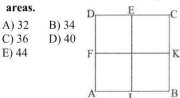

12) ABCD and KFEL are the squares. A(ABCD)=289cm², A(KFEL)=400cm². Find the ratio perimeter.

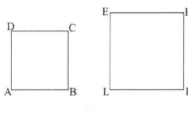

A) $\dfrac{18}{17}$ B) $\dfrac{21}{17}$ C) $\dfrac{17}{20}$

D) $\dfrac{19}{20}$ E) $\dfrac{20}{13}$

13) ABCD and EFKL are the squares. AB=12cm. EF=6cm. Find the drawn area.

A) 96
B) 100
C) 108
D) 112
E) 120

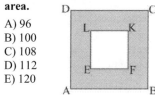

14) ABCD and EFKL are the squares. Perimeter ABCD is $8\sqrt{3}$cm and perimeter EFKL is the $4\sqrt{2}$ cm. Find the area ratio.

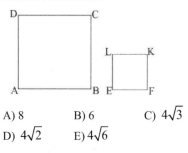

A) 8   B) 6   C) $4\sqrt{3}$

D) $4\sqrt{2}$ E) $4\sqrt{6}$

15) ABCD and LKFE are squares. DB=14cm, FL=8cm. Find the area ratio.

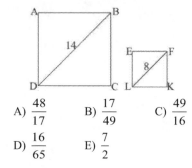

A) $\dfrac{48}{17}$ B) $\dfrac{17}{49}$ C) $\dfrac{49}{16}$

D) $\dfrac{16}{65}$ E) $\dfrac{7}{2}$

TEST – 16
(Area and Perimeter of the Rectangle)

1) ABCD is the rectangle. AB=x+4, BC=x+2, Find the perimeter of ABCD.

   A) 4x+8
   B) 4x+10
   C) 4x+12
   D) 4x+4
   E) 12x+4

2) ABCD is the rectangle. AB=3x, BC=2x, perimeter ABCD is 30cm. Find the area of ABCD.

   A) 54
   B) 58
   C) 60
   D) 64
   E) 68

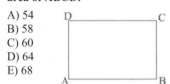

3) ABCD is the rectangle. AB=10, BC=6. Find the ratio A(ABCD):P(ABCD).

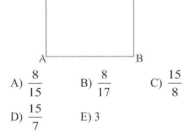

   A) $\dfrac{8}{15}$ B) $\dfrac{8}{17}$ C) $\dfrac{15}{8}$

   D) $\dfrac{15}{7}$ E) 3

4) ABCD is the rectangle. Area of ABCD is the 18cm². Find the perimeter of ABCD.

   A) 10
   B) 12
   C) 14
   D) 15
   E) 18

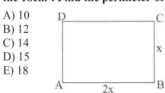

5) ABCD is the rectangle. BC=5, AC=13. Find the perimeter of ABCD.

   A) 32
   B) 33
   C) 34
   D) 36
   E) 48

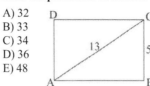

6) ABCD is the rectangle. BC=12, AB=16. P(ABCD):P(BAC).

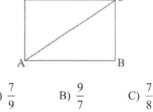

   A) $\dfrac{7}{9}$ B) $\dfrac{9}{7}$ C) $\dfrac{7}{8}$

   D) $\dfrac{7}{6}$ E) $\dfrac{6}{7}$

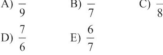

7) AB=10, BC=8, A(ABCD):A(ABC)=?

   A) 1
   B) 2
   C) 3
   D) 4
   E) $\dfrac{2}{3}$

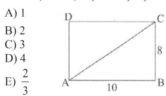

8) A rectangle has edges with lengths of 5cm and 3cm. Find the length of a diagonal of the rectangle.

   A) 34   B) 17   C) $\sqrt{34}$

   D) $\sqrt{32}$ E) $\sqrt{37}$

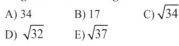

9) The lengths of two sides of a rectangle are in the ratio 1:3. Find the area of the rectangle if its perimeter is 200cm.

A) 1775   B) 1875
C) 1880   D) 1475
E) 1980

0) AE=3, EC=8, ∠DEC=90°, Find the DE?

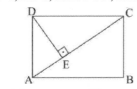

A) $\sqrt{6}$ B) $2\sqrt{6}$ C) $2\sqrt{3}$

D) $2\sqrt{5}$ E) 4

11) AB=4, BC=3, DC=5. Find the ratio A(ABD):A(BCD)?

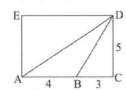

A) $\dfrac{4}{3}$ B) $\dfrac{3}{4}$ C) $\dfrac{5}{3}$

D) $\dfrac{3}{5}$ E) $\dfrac{4}{5}$

12) ABCD is the rectangle. AB=5, BC=8. Area of ABD=10cm². Find the area of A(ACDE)?

 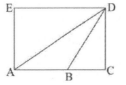

A) 30
B) 32
C) 34
D) 36
E) 52

13) ABCD and LEFK are rectangles. AB=m, BC=n, LE=x, EF=y. Find the striped area.

A) xy
B) mn
C) mn+xy
D) mn–xy
E) xy–mn

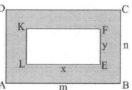

14) ABCD and EFKL are rectangles. AB=2m, BC=2n, EF=m, KF=n. Find the ratio perimeter P(ABCD) : P(LEFK).

A) 1
B) 2
C) 2m+2n
D) m+n
E) 2m+3n

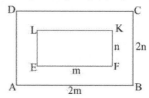

15) ABCD is the rectangle. AE=EC. Find the ∠CEB.

A) 23
B) 24
C) 46
D) 50
E) 54

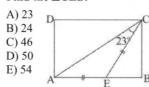

TEST – 17
(Area and Perimeter of the Parallelogram)

1) ABCD is the parallelogram. $\angle BDC=34^{\circ}$, $\angle ADB=74^{\circ}$, Find the $\angle ABC$.

A) 104
B) 106
C) 108
D) 110
E) 112

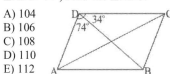

5) ABCD is the parallelogram. AB=4x–4, DC=24. Find the $(2x^2+2)$.

A) 106
B) 104
C) 102
D) 100
E) 98

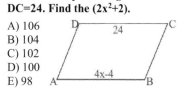

2) ABCD is the parallelogram. AB=x, DC=12, BC=m, AD=7, AE=6 if (x+m+a)=?

A) 30
B) 29
C) 28
D) 27
E) 25

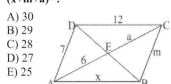

6) Finf the area of the parallelogram with base 13cm and height 6cm.

A) 78   B) 74   C) 68
D) 64   E) 60

3) ABCD is the parallelogram. AB=3y, DC=18, AD=8, BC=3x–4. Find the x+y=?

A) 9
B) 10
C) 11
D) 12
E) 13

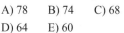

7) ABCD is the parallelogram. AB=10, ED=4. Find the area of ABCD.

A) 20
B) 30
C) 36
D) 40
E) 80

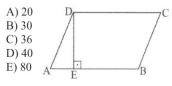

4) ABCD is the parallelogram. $\angle A=3x^{\circ}$, $\angle D=6x^{\circ}$, x=?

A) 40
B) 36
C) 30
D) 25
E) 20

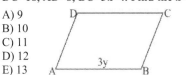

8) ABCD is the parallelogram. BC=8cm, DE=12cm, AB=11cm, Find the area of ABCD.

A) 44
B) 88
C) 96
D) 98
E) 100

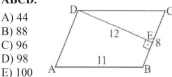

9) ABCD is the parallelogram. AB=16cm, DE=10cm, DF=14cm, AD=?

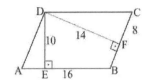

A) $\dfrac{80}{9}$ B) $\dfrac{90}{8}$ C) $\dfrac{80}{14}$

D) $\dfrac{80}{7}$ E) $\dfrac{80}{17}$

10) ABCD is the parallelogram. $\angle A=66^0$. Evaluate x–y.

A) 50
B) 48
C) 46
D) 44
E) 42

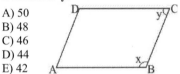

11) The ratio of the side of a parallelogram is 11:13. What is the least possible integer value of its perimeter?

A) 48   B) 44   C) 40

D) 36   E) 32

12) ABCD is the parallelogram. A(ADE)=9cm². Find the area of ABCD.

A) 36
B) 27
C) 18
D) 16
E) 9

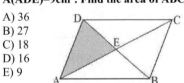

13) Find the area of the parallelogram with base 14cm and height $2\sqrt{3}$ cm.

A) 28   B) 20   C) $28\sqrt{2}$

D) $28\sqrt{3}$ E) $56\sqrt{3}$

14) ABCD is the parallelogram. AK=12, BK=7. Find the ratio $\dfrac{AC}{BD}=?$

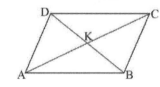

A) $\dfrac{12}{5}$ B) $\dfrac{13}{6}$ C) $\dfrac{12}{7}$

D) $\dfrac{13}{7}$ E) 2

15) ABCD is the parallelogram. $\dfrac{AB}{BC}=\dfrac{1}{3}$. Perimeter ABCD is the 60cm. Find the AB.

A) 10
B) 8.5
C) 7
D) 7.5
E) 6

TEST – 18
(Area and Perimeter of the Rhombus)

1) Find the perimeter of rhombus with edge length 13cm.

A) 26   B) 39   C) 42
D) 52   E) 62

2) Rhomb perimeter is 60cm. Find the side of rhombus

A) 12   B) 13   C) 14
D) 15   E) 20

3) Rhomb perimeter is $(4\pi-4)$cm, Find the side of rhombus

A) 4π B) 4   C) $2\pi-2$
D) $\pi-1$ E) $2\pi-4$

4) Find the area of a rhombus with diagonal lengths 10cm and 14cm.

A) 140   B) 130   C) 100
D) 70   E) 80

5) Rhomb perimeter is 4^{m+1}cm. Find the side of rhombus

A) 4   B) 4^m C) 2
D) 2^m E) 1

6) Find the perimeter of rhombus with diagonal lengths 12cm and 16cm.

A) 20   B) 25   C) 30
D) 35   E) 40

7) The side length of a rhombus is $10\sqrt{2}$ cm. Find the area of the rhombus if its smaller angle is 45º.

A) $50\sqrt{2}$ B) $60\sqrt{2}$
C) $70\sqrt{2}$ D) $80\sqrt{2}$
E) $100\sqrt{2}$

8) The diagonal length of a rhombus are 10cm and 24cm. Find the side of rhombus?

A) 13   B) 12   C) $\dfrac{13}{2}$ D) 6   E) 7

9) Find the side of a rhombus with diagonal lengths 36cm and 48cm.

A) 30   B) 24   C) 20

D) 18   E) 15

10) ABCD is the rhombus. AC=12, BD=6, BC=?

A) $5\sqrt{3}$ B) $3\sqrt{5}$

C) $4\sqrt{3}$ D) $3\sqrt{4}$

E) 5

11) ABCD is the rhombus. BC=8cm, EF=9cm, ∠DFE=90°. Find the area of ABCD?

A) 63
B) 72
C) 70
D) 64
E) 60

12) Find the area of a rhombus with side lengths 12 and altitude 9cm.

A) 108   B) 144   C) 106

D) 107   E) 110

13) Find the area of a rhombus with side lengths $4\sqrt{3}$ and altitude 5cm.

A) $10\sqrt{2}$ B) $20\sqrt{2}$ C) $20\sqrt{3}$

D) 20   E) 40

14) Find the perimeter of a rhombus with diagonal lengths 12cm and 8cm.

A) $3\sqrt{3}$ B) $4\sqrt{3}$ C) $6\sqrt{3}$

D) $8\sqrt{13}$ E) $10\sqrt{3}$

15) The rhombus area is $20\sqrt{3}\,cm^2$. The side is 10cm. Find the altitude of the rhombus.

A) $\sqrt{3}$ B) $2\sqrt{2}$ C) $2\sqrt{3}$

D) $4\sqrt{3}$ E) $4\sqrt{5}$

TEST – 19
(Rigid motion in a Plane and Reflections)

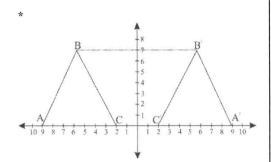

*

1) **Find the coordinate A$^/$=?**

   A) (9, 0)   B) (8, 0)

   C) (7, 6)   D) (0, 9)

   E) (0, 8)

2) **Find the coordinate B$^/$=?**

   A) (6, 6)   B) (6, 7)

   C) (7, 6)   D) (7, 8)

   E) (7, 4)

*   **Reflection in the line x=4, a flip over the line x=4.**

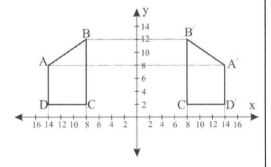

3) **A$^/$=?**

   A) (14, 12)   B) (12, 14)

   C) (14, 8)   D) (10, 8)

   E) (9, 8)

4) **B$^/$=?**

   A) (8, 2)   B) (8, 4)

   C) (8, 12)   D) (12, 8)

   E) (12, 4)

5) **If K(4, 8) is reflected in the line y=4, then K$^/$=?**

   A) (4, 2)   B) (4, 6)

   C) (4, 8)   D) (4, 0)

   E) (0, 4)

6) **If N(12, –4) is reflected in the line x=6, then N$^/$=?**

   A) (0, 4)   B) (0, –4)

   C) (4, 0)   D) (–4, 0)

   E) (6, –2)

7) **If A(7, 4) is reflected in the line x=2, then A$^/$=?**

   A) (3, 3)   B) (3, –3)

   C) (–3, 3)   D) (–3, 4)

   E) (6, 4)

*   **Given that the diagram shows a reflection in a line**

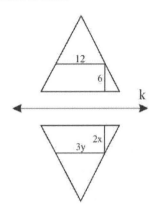

8)   y=?

   A) 1   B) 2   C) 3   D) 4   E) 6

9)   x+y=?

   A) 10   B) 9   C) 8   D) 7   E) 6

*   **Given that the diagram shows a reflection in a line:**

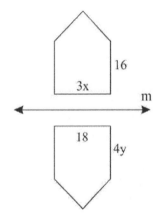

10)   x=?

   A) 10   B) 9   C) 8   D) 7   E) 6

11)   2y+2x=?

   A) 20   B) 19   C) 18
   D) 17   E) 16

12)   Find the coordinates of A(8, 4) reflected in the line y=2.

   A) (8, 4)   B) (8, 1)
   C) (8, 0)   D) (0, 8)
   E) (0, 4)

13)   Find the coordinates of M(–4, 10) reflected in the y–axis. M′=?

   A) (4, 10)   B) (–4, 10)
   C) (10, 4)   D) (–10, 4)
   E) (4, 8)

14)   Find the coordinates of M′(–3, 7) reflected in the x–axis. M′=?

   A) (3, 3)   B) (3, 4)
   C) (7, 4)   D) (3, 7)
   E) (–3, –7)

15)   Find the coordinates of N(4, 3) reflected B(0, 0). N′=?

   A) (–3, –4)   B) (–3, 4)
   C) (–4, 3)   D) (–4, –3)
   E) (–3, 6)

TEST – 20
(Translation and Vectors)

* **Use coordinate notation to describe the translation.**

1) **7 units to the right and 5 units down.**
    (x, y) →?
    A) (x+7, y–5)   B) (x+7, y–3)
    C) (x+3, y–7)   D) (x+3, y+7)
    E) (x–3, y+4)

2) **6 units up and 12 units to the right.**
    (x, y) →?
    A) (x+12, y+6)   B) (x–6, y–12)
    C) (x+6, y+12)   D) (x+6, y+6)
    E) (x+12, y+4)

3) **10 units down and 7 units to the left.**
    (x, y) →?
    A) (x+10, y+7)   B) (x–10, y–10)
    C) (x–7, y–10)   D) (x+6, y+6)
    E) (x–10, y–7)

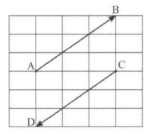

* **Name the vector and write its component form.**

4) A) $\overrightarrow{AB}$; (4, 2)   B) $\overrightarrow{AB}$; (3, 3)
    C) $\overrightarrow{AB}$; (2, 4)   D) $\overrightarrow{AB}$; (3, –3)
    E) $\overrightarrow{AB}$; (–2, –2)

5) A) $\overrightarrow{CD}$; (–3, –3)   B) $\overrightarrow{CD}$; (3, 3)
    C) $\overrightarrow{CD}$; (4, 3)   D) $\overrightarrow{CD}$; (–3, 3)
    E) $\overrightarrow{CD}$; (2, –3)

6) **(x, y) →? Where is x and y locate?**

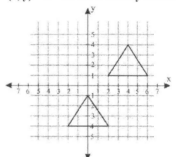

    A) (x–3, y+4)   B) (x–4, y–5)
    C) (x+3, y–5)   D) (x–2, y+5)
    E) (x+2, y+4)

7) **Consider the translation that defined by the coordinate notation**
    (x, y)→(x+5, y–4). What is the image of (3, 6)?
    A) (8, 4)   B) (8, 0)   C) (8, 3)
    D) (8, 2)   E) (2, 8)

8) **(x, y) → (x+7, y+3). What is the image of (3, 4)?**
    A) (10, 7)   B) (10, 6)   C) (7, 10)
    D) (8, 5)   E) (8, 6)

9)   (x, y) → (x+4, y+4). The point (6, 8) will
     be?

   A) (10, 4)   B) (10, 2)   C) (12, 10)
   D) (10, 9)   E) (10, 12)

10) Vector translation of (x, y) →?

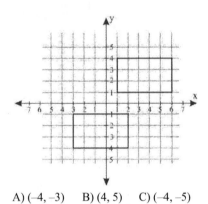

   A) (−4, −3)   B) (4, 5)   C) (−4, −5)
   D) (−4, −6)   E) (−5, −4)

11) The vector A(-4, -2) is translated 5 units
     right and 10 units down. What is the
     coordinates of end point?

   A) (1, 12)   B) (1, -12)   C) (2, 12)
   D) (3, 10)   E) (6, 8)

12) Describe the translation 6 units to the
     left and 8 unit up using a vector.

   A) (-6, 8)   B) (-6, -8)   C) (-8, 6)
   D) (-6, 7)   E) (-8, -6)

13) Describe in words the distance and
     direction of the translation represented
     by the vector <6, -14>.

   A) 6 unit down and 14 units up
   B) 6 unit right and 14 units down
   C) 14 unit left and 6 units down
   D) 6 unit left and 14 units down
   E) 14 unit up and 6 unit down

14) Use the translation (x, y) → (x+4, y-2).
     What is the image of A(8, 10)?

   A) (9, 8)   B) (12, 10)   C) (10, 8)
   D) (8, 12)   E) (12, 8)

15) Use the translation (x, y) → (x-6, y+2).
     A(13, -4)→?

   A) (-12, 10)   B) (-12, 4)   C) (7, 2)
   D) (7, -2)   E) (-2, 7)

TEST – 21
(Similar Triangles)

1) In the diagram: $\triangle ABC \sim \triangle DEC$, DE=4, AB=16, AC=24. Find the DC=?

A) 6
B) 7
C) 8
D) 9
E) 4,8

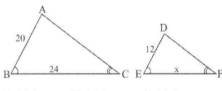

2) The triangles shown are similar. Find the x.

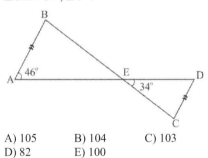

A) 16.4   B) 15.4   C) 14.4
D) 13.3   E) 12.7

3) AB||DC and ∠A=46º, ∠CED=34º, ∠C=?

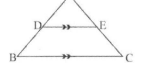

A) 105   B) 104   C) 103
D) 82   E) 100

4) DE||BC and AD=6, DB=9, EC=12, AE=?

A) 11
B) 10
C) 9
D) 8
E) 7

5) AD=10, BD=16, AC=24, EC=?

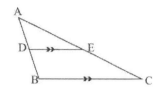

A) $\frac{192}{13}$ B) $\frac{191}{12}$ C) $\frac{189}{13}$

D) $\frac{188}{15}$ E) $\frac{182}{13}$

6) AD=24, DB=16, BC=28, ED=?

A) $\frac{57}{3}$

B) $\frac{57}{4}$

C) $\frac{56}{3}$

D) $\frac{56}{5}$

E) 4.2

7) x =?

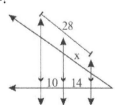

A) $\frac{29}{4}$ B) $\frac{29}{2}$ C) $\frac{39}{4}$

D) $\frac{39}{5}$ E) $\frac{49}{3}$

8) x =?

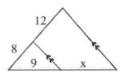

A) $\dfrac{27}{2}$ B) $\dfrac{23}{4}$ C) $\dfrac{33}{5}$

D) $\dfrac{33}{2}$ E) $\dfrac{33}{4}$

9) BC=5, EF=3, ABC~DEF.
    Find the ratio A(ABC):A(DEF).

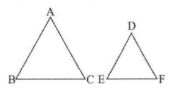

A) $\dfrac{5}{3}$ B) $\dfrac{3}{5}$ C) $\dfrac{25}{3}$

D) $\dfrac{3}{25}$ E) $\dfrac{25}{9}$

0) △ABC~△DEF, BC=2cm,
    A(ABC)=4cm², EF=5cm, S(DEF)=?

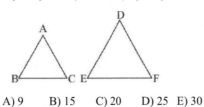

A) 9   B) 15   C) 20   D) 25   E) 30

11) △ABC~△EDC, x =?

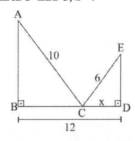

A) $\dfrac{9}{2}$ B) $\dfrac{9}{4}$ C) $\dfrac{8}{3}$ D) $\dfrac{7}{2}$ E) 5

12) AD=12, DC=16, BC=18, BE=?

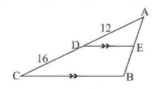

A) 3   B) 4   C) 5

D) 4.5   E) 7.7

13) DE||BC, DE is the midsegment.
    A(ADE)=5cm² if A(ABC)=?

A) 15
B) 20
C) 22
D) 24
E) 25

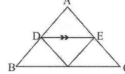

14) DE and FE are the midpoint segments.
    DE=6cm, FE=4cm, AB+BC=?

A) 20
B) 18
C) 17
D) 16
E) 15

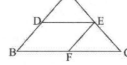

15) AE=3, AC=6. Find the relationship
    between x and y.

A) x=y
B) x=2y
C) x=3y
D) y=2x
E) y=3x

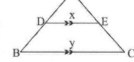

TEST – 22
(The Pythagorean Theorem)

1) **Find the length of a hypotenuse, x=?**

A) $\sqrt{43}$

B) $\sqrt{55}$

C) $\sqrt{65}$

D) $\sqrt{66}$

E) $\sqrt{72}$

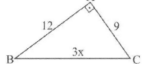

2) **∠A=90°, AB=12, AC=9, (2x+2)=?**

A) 10
B) 11
C) 12
D) 13
E) 14

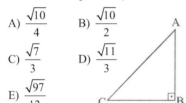

3) **∠B=90°, AB=$\frac{1}{3}$, BC=$\frac{3}{4}$, AC=?**

A) $\frac{\sqrt{10}}{4}$ B) $\frac{\sqrt{10}}{2}$

C) $\frac{\sqrt{7}}{3}$ D) $\frac{\sqrt{11}}{3}$

E) $\frac{\sqrt{97}}{12}$

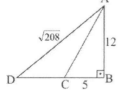

4) **∠B=90°, AD=$\sqrt{208}$, AB=12, BC=5, DC=?**

A) 3
B) 4
C) 5
D) 6
E) 7

5) **AE=5, EC=3, BC=2, AB=?**

A) $\sqrt{10}$

B) $\sqrt{12}$

C) $\sqrt{20}$

D) $\sqrt{25}$

E) $\sqrt{30}$

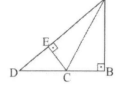

6) **∠B=90°, AC=4x, AB=3x, BC=?**

A) 5
B) 5x
C) 5x²
D) 25x²
E) $x\sqrt{7}$

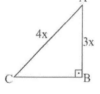

7) **∠B=90°, AB=2x, BC=6x, P(ABC)=?**

A) 10x
B) 12x
C) $2x\sqrt{10}$
D) $2x\sqrt{10} +8x$
E) $2\sqrt{10x} + 8x$

8) **AB=6, BD=4, DC=2, ∠ADC=90°, AC=x=?**

A) $\sqrt{23}$

B) $2\sqrt{3}$

C) $3\sqrt{2}$

D) $2\sqrt{5}$

E) $2\sqrt{6}$

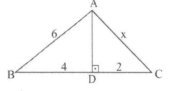

9) ∠ADC=90º, AB=6, AD=4, AC=7,
BD:DC=?

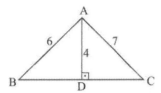

A) $\dfrac{2\sqrt{5}}{3}$ B) $\dfrac{2\sqrt{5}}{\sqrt{11}}$ C) $\dfrac{2\sqrt{5}}{\sqrt{33}}$

D) $\dfrac{3\sqrt{5}}{\sqrt{11}}$ E) $\dfrac{4\sqrt{5}}{\sqrt{33}}$

10) ∠A=∠D=90º, BD=5,   DC=8,
$\dfrac{AD}{A(ABC)}=?$

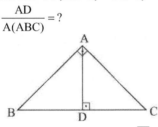

A) $\dfrac{2}{\sqrt{10}}$ B) $\dfrac{2}{9}$ C) $\dfrac{\sqrt{10}}{2}$

D) $\dfrac{\sqrt{5}}{\sqrt{13}}$ E) $\dfrac{2}{13}$

11) ∠A=∠D=90º, BD=3x, DC=4x, AB:AC=?

A) $\sqrt{3}$ B) $\dfrac{\sqrt{3}}{2}$

C) $\dfrac{2}{\sqrt{3}}$ D) $\dfrac{\sqrt{5}}{2}$

E) $\dfrac{\sqrt{5}}{3}$

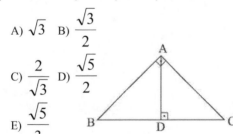

12) ∠B=90º, AB=a, BC=4a. Find the
perimeter △ABC?

A) $4a+\sqrt{17}$

B) $5a+\sqrt{17}$

C) $5a+a\sqrt{17}$

D) $6a+\sqrt{17}$

E) $6a+a\sqrt{17}$

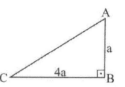

13) ∠B=90º, AC=6x, AB=3x, $\dfrac{BC}{P(ABC)}=?$

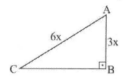

A) $\dfrac{\sqrt{3}}{3+\sqrt{3}}$ B) $\dfrac{3}{3-\sqrt{3}}$

C) $\dfrac{4}{4+4\sqrt{3}}$ D) $\dfrac{5}{2+\sqrt{3}}$

E) $\dfrac{3}{2+\sqrt{3}}$

14) ∠B=90º, AB=3, BC=7, $\dfrac{AC}{A(ABC)}=?$

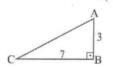

A) $\dfrac{2\sqrt{58}}{21}$ B) $\dfrac{3\sqrt{47}}{21}$

C) $\dfrac{4\sqrt{58}}{2}$ D) $\dfrac{6\sqrt{29}}{5}$

E) $\sqrt{58}+3$

15) ∠A=∠D=90º, BD=4a, DC=6a, AD=?

A) $2\sqrt{6}$

B) $3\sqrt{6}\,a$

C) $2\sqrt{5}\,a$

D) $a\,2\sqrt{6}$

E) $a\cdot2\sqrt{7}\,a$

TEST – 23
(Special Right Triangle)

(Theorem: 45° – 45° – 90°)
(Theorem: 30° – 30° – 90°)

1) ∠B=90°, AB=BC=5, AC=?

A) $5\sqrt{3}$ B) $5\sqrt{2}$

C) $5\sqrt{4}$ D) 6

E) 7

2) ∠B=90°, ∠A=∠C=45°, AC= $7\sqrt{2}$,
AB+BC=?

A) 9   B) 10

C) 11   D) 12

E) 14

3) ∠B=90°, AC=14, ∠A=∠C=45°,
A(ABC)=?

A) 49   B) 48

C) 44   D) 40

E) 36

4) ∠B=90°, AB=BC=3x, $\dfrac{P(ABC)}{AC}=?$

A) $2+\sqrt{2}$ B) $3+\sqrt{3}$

C) $3+\sqrt{2}$ D) $\dfrac{3+\sqrt{3}}{3}$

E) $\dfrac{2+\sqrt{2}}{2}$

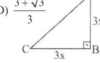

5) ∠B=90°, ∠A=∠C=45°, A(ABC)=10cm².
Find the perimeter of ABC.

A) $6\sqrt{5}$ B) $2\sqrt{5}+2\sqrt{10}$

C) $2\sqrt{10}+4\sqrt{5}$ D) $6+2\sqrt{5}$

E) $2\sqrt{10}+8$

6) ∠A=90°, ∠B=∠C=45°, BC=20cm,
$\dfrac{(AB+AC)}{BC}=?$

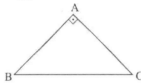

A) $\sqrt{2}$ B) $\sqrt{3}$ C) $2\sqrt{2}$

D) $3\sqrt{3}$ E) 4

7) ∠A=60°, ∠B=90°, ∠C=30°, AC=18cm,
$\dfrac{BC}{AB}=?$

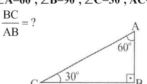

A) 2   B) 3   C) $2\sqrt{2}$

D) $3\sqrt{3}$ E) $\sqrt{3}$

8) ∠A=60°, ∠B=90°, AB=8cm, Find the
area of △ABC.

A) $32\sqrt{3}$ B) 32

C) 16   D) $16\sqrt{3}$

E) 24

9) ∠A=60°, ∠B=90°, AC=6x, Find the area of △ABC.

A) $9x^2$

B) $\dfrac{9\sqrt{3}}{2}$

C) $\dfrac{6x^2}{5}$

D) $\dfrac{9x\sqrt{3}}{2}$

E) $\dfrac{9x^2\sqrt{3}}{2}$

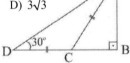

A) $\dfrac{36}{7}$ B) $\dfrac{36}{8}$

C) 6   D) 7

E) $\dfrac{36}{5}$

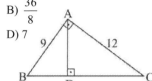

10) ∠B=90°, ∠D=30°, DC=AC=4, BC=?

A) 2   B) $2\sqrt{3}$

C) 3   D) $3\sqrt{3}$

E) 4

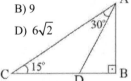

14) ∠B=90°, BC=BD, DC=4, AD=2, $\dfrac{AB}{BC}=?$

A) $\sqrt{3}+1$ B) $\sqrt{3}-1$

C) $\dfrac{1+\sqrt{2}}{\sqrt{2}}$ D) $2\sqrt{2}+2$

E) $\sqrt{2}+1$

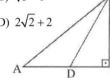

11) ∠B=90°, ∠C=15°, ∠DAB=30°, AB=6, AD=?

A) 12   B) 9

C) $6\sqrt{3}$ D) $6\sqrt{2}$

E) $6\sqrt{5}$

15) ∠B=90°, AB=3x, BC=3y, AC=?

A) $3\sqrt{x^2+y^2}$

B) $9x^2+9y^2$

C) $9\sqrt{x+y}$

D) $9\sqrt{x^2+y^2}$

E) $3x+3y$

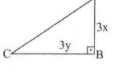

12) ∠C=90°, ∠BAC=45°, ∠CAD=30°, AD=6, AB=?

A) 6   B) $6\sqrt{2}$

C) $3\sqrt{2}$ D) $3\sqrt{3}$

E) $3\sqrt{6}$

13) ∠A=∠D=90°, AB=9, AC=12, AD=?

TEST – 24
(Vectors)

1) If $\vec{A} = (2i + 4j)$ and $\vec{B} = (3i + 3j)$ the result vector of $3\vec{A} + 2\vec{B}$ equals.

A) 12i+18j   B) 18i+21j
C) 17i+17j   D) 8i+8j
E) 20i+21j

2) Suppose $\vec{A} = (6, 5), \ \vec{B} = (9, \ 1)$, Find the magnitude of $\vec{A} - \vec{B}$.

A) 3   B) 4   C) 5   D) 6   E) 7

3) Consider the car time graph shown. Find the area from 4 to 8 is most nearly.

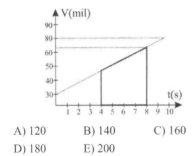

A) 120   B) 140   C) 160
D) 180   E) 200

4) Let it i, j and k be unit vectors in the x, y and z directions. Suppose that

$\vec{A} = 4i - 2j + 3k$. What is the magnitude of the vector A?

A) 12   B) $\sqrt{12}$ C) 24
D) $\sqrt{24}$ E) $\sqrt{29}$

5) Relative to the origin point A has a position vector 2i-2j and B has position vector 4i+6j. What is $\overrightarrow{AB}$?

A) 6i+8j   B) 6i–4j
C) 2i+8j   D) 8i+6j
E) 10i+8j

6) Let i and j be unit vectors in the x and y directions respectively. Suppose that A=6i–8j. What is the magnitude of the vector A?

A) 14   B) 13   C) 12
D) 11   E) 10

7 Let $\vec{A} = (-6, \ 4)$ and $\vec{B} = (7, \ 5)$. Write the component form of the sum $\vec{A} + \vec{B}$.

A) (–4, 9)   B) (–13, 9)
C) (1, 9)   D) (–1, 9)
E) (3, 4)

8) What is the magnitude of the vector $\vec{A} = (3, \ 5)$?

A) 24   B) $\sqrt{24}$ C) 34
D) $\sqrt{34}$ E) 6

9) Multiply the vector $\vec{A} = (9, 4)$ by the scalar 5.

A) (18, 8) B) (36, 20)

C) (36, 16) D) (20, 36)

E) (45, 20)

10) Add the vectors $\vec{A} = (1, 2, 3)$ and $\vec{B} = (4, 5, 6)$.

A) (5, 7, 9) B) (5, 7, 8)

C) (6, 7, 9) D) (6, 7, 10)

E) (9, 8, 12)

11) What is the magnitude of the vector $\vec{B} = (2; -3; -4)$?

A) 29 B) $\sqrt{29}$ C) 26

D) $\sqrt{26}$ E) 6

12) $\vec{A} = (5, 4, 3)$, $\vec{B} = (1, 2, 3)$ and $\vec{C} = 2\vec{A} - 3\vec{B}$. What is the magnitude of $\vec{C}$?

A) $\sqrt{32}$ B) $\sqrt{42}$ C) $\sqrt{52}$

D) $\sqrt{62}$ E) $\sqrt{72}$

13) If $\vec{A} = (6, 4)$ and $\vec{B} = (-4, -2)$. What is the $\vec{A} + \vec{B}$?

A) (10, 2) B) (10, -2)

C) (2, 2) D) (-2, -2)

E) (3, 6)

14) Find the $\vec{A} + \vec{B}$?

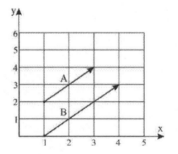

A) (3, 3) B) (3, 5) C) (5, 3)

D) (4, 4) E) (5, 5)

15) Find the $\vec{A} + \vec{B} + \vec{C}$?

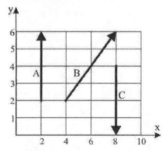

A) (6, 6) B) (7, 7) C) (6, 8)

D) (8, 6) E) (4, 4)

TEST – 25
(Equations of Circle)

1) **Circle with center (0, 0), radius 7. Find the formula.**

   A) $x^2+y^2=7$ B) $x^2+y^2=14$

   C) $x^2+y^2=49$ D) $x^2+y^2=\sqrt{7}$

   E) $x^2+y^2=\sqrt{14}$

2) **Circle with center (3, –6), radius 4. Find the formula.**

   A) $(x–2)^2+(y+6)^2=8$

   B) $(x–3)^2+(y–6)^2=16$

   C) $(x+3)^2+(y+6)^2=16$

   D) $(x–3)^2+(y+6)^2=16$

   E) $x^2+y^2=16$

3) **$x^2+y^2+8x+10y+12=0$. Find the circle center coordinate.**

   A) (8, 10) B) (–8, 10)

   C) (–4, –5) D) (4, 5)

   E) (8, 12)

4) **$2x^2+2y^2+8x–10y+14=0$. Find the circle center coordinate.**

   A) $\left(2, \dfrac{5}{2}\right)$ B) $\left(-2, \dfrac{5}{2}\right)$

   C) $\left(\dfrac{5}{2}, 2\right)$ D) $\left(2, -\dfrac{5}{2}\right)$

   E) (–2, 4)

5) **Write the equation for the circle shown below if it is shifted 2 units to the right and 3 units up.**

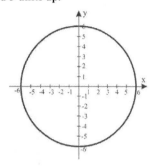

   A) $(x–2)^2+(y–3)^2=6$
   B) $(x–2)^2+(y–3)^2=36$
   C) $(x–2)^2+(y+3)^2=6$
   D) $(x+2)^2+(y–3)^2=36$
   E) $(x+2)^2+(y+3)^2=18$

6) **$(x–6)^2+(y–5)^2=36$. Find the circle center coordinate.**

   A) (–6, 5) B) (–6, –5)

   C) (6, 5) D) (5, 6)

   E) (–5, –6)

7) **$(x–3)^2+(y–4)^2=25$. Find the radius.**

   A) 3 B) 4 C) 5 D) 10 E) 25

8) **Find the equation of the circle in general form.**

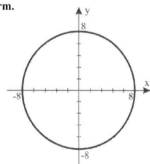

   A) $x^2+y^2=64$ B) $x^2+y^2=36$
   C) $x^2+y^2=8$ D) $x^2+y^2=\sqrt{8}$
   E) $x^2+y^2+64=0$

9) A circle has center (4, –5) and the point (–2, –9) lies on the circumference of the circle. What is the equation of the circle in standard form.

A) $(x–4)^2+(y–5)^2=26$

B) $(x–4)^2+(y+5)^2=52$
C) $(x+4)^2+(y+5)^2=26$
D) $(x–3)^2+(y+5)^2=52$
E) $(x–4)^2+(y+6)^2=26$

10) A circle has center (–8, 12) and the point (5, –2) lies on the circumference of the circle. What is the equation of the circle in standard form.

A) $(x+8)^2+(y–12)^2=\sqrt{313}$

B) $(x+8)^2+(y+12)^2=\sqrt{313}$
C) $(x–8)^2+(y+12)^2=313$
D) $(x–8)^2+(y–10)^2=313$
E) $(x+8)^2+(y–12)^2=365$

11) What is the center of circle: $(x–6)^2+(y+2)^2=64$

A) $(–6, –2)$ B) $(6, –3)$
C) $(2, –6)$ D) $(2, 6)$
E) $(6, –2)$

12) What is the radius of circle $(x+3)^2+(y-3)^2=25$?

A) 3   B) 2   C) 4   D) 5   E) 6

13) What is the centre of the circle $x^2+y^2+16x-24y+56=0$?

A) (16, -24)   B) (16, -12)
C) (8, –12)   D) (-8, 12)
E) (-8, -12)

14) What is the radius of circle $x^2+y^2-7x+13y-20=0$?

A) $\sqrt{298}$ B) $2\sqrt{298}$

C) $\dfrac{\sqrt{298}}{2}$ D) $\dfrac{\sqrt{198}}{2}$

E) $\dfrac{\sqrt{198}}{3}$

15) $x^2+y^2=81$, r=?
A) 11
B) 10
C) 9
D) 8
E) 3

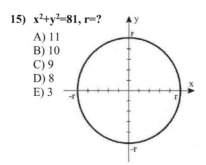

TEST – 26
(Angle measures in Polygon)

1) How many side does a polygon have if the sum of its interior angle is 540°?

   A) 8   B) 7   C) 6   D) 5   E) 4

2) How many side does a polygon have if the sum of its interior angle is 1440°?

   A) 12   B) 11   C) 10   D) 9   E) 8

3) What is the size of one interior angle of a regular eighteen-side polygon?

   A) 170   B) 160   C) 150
   D) 140   E) 130

4) Each of the interior angle of a regular polygon is 160°. How many sides does the polygon have?

   A) 20   B) 18   C) 16
   D) 14   E) 12

5) What is the sum of the interior angles of a regular fourteen–sided polygon?

   A) 1800   B) 1900   C) 2000
   D) 2160   E) 2260

6) ∠A=60°, ∠B=110°, ∠C=114°, ∠D=20°, x=?

   A) 110
   B) 114
   C) 120
   D) 122
   E) 124

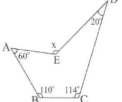

7) What is the measure of each interior angle in a regular hexagon?

   A) 45   B) 60   C) 75
   D) 100   E) 120

8) A regular polygon with an exterior angle of 30°. Find the sides?

   A) 10   B) 11   C) 12
   D) 13   E) 14

9) The sum of the measures of the interior angles of a dodecagon (side is 12)?

A) 1160   B) 1060   C) 1888

D) 1800   E) 2160

10) α=?

A) 45
B) 50
C) 55
D) 60
E) 70

11) x=?

A) 91
B) 101
C) 111
D) 121
E) 124

12) AB=BC=DC=DE=EF=FA=10cm, α=?

A) 30
B) 36
C) 40
D) 60
E) 70

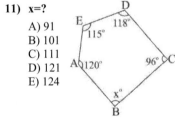

13) x=?

A) 110
B) 115
C) 120
D) 124
E) 125

14) Find the perimeter of regular hexagon if one side is 10cm?

A) 24   B) 30   C) 36

D) 40   E) 60

15) Find the area of regular hexagon if one side is 10cm?

A) 150   B) $150\sqrt{2}$ C) $150\sqrt{3}$

D) 160   E) $160\sqrt{3}$

TEST – 27
(Tangents to Circle)

1) $\overleftrightarrow{AB}$ is tangent to ⊙M at A. $\overleftrightarrow{BC}$ is tangent to ⊙M at C, x=?

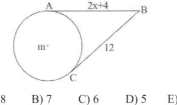

A) 8   B) 7   C) 6   D) 5   E) 4

2)   AB=x²–6, BC=30. Find the value of x.

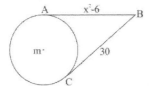

A) 6²   B) 4   C) 6
D) 12   E) –12

3)   AB=11, BC=x. Find the value of x.

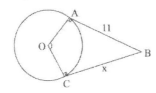

A) 22   B) 18   C) 15
D) 14   E) 11

4)   AB=4x, BC=20. Find the value of x.

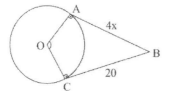

A) 5   B) 6   C) 7   D) 8   E) 10

5)   AB=3x+6, BC=2x+12. Find the value of x.

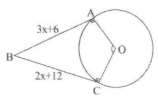

A) 10   B) 9   C) 8   D) 7   E) 6

6)   AB=x²–9, BC=40. Find the value of x.

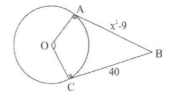

A) ±6   B) 7   C) ±5   D) 8   E) 9

7)   AB=8, AD=6, BC=? D is the centre of circle.

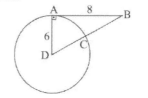

A) 1   B) 2   C) 3   D) 4   E) 5

8)   AD=r=9, BC=6, AB=?

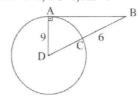

A) 14   B) 13   C) 12
D) 11   E) 10

59

9) **O is the center of circle. AB=20, BC=12. r=?**

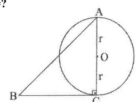

A) 8   B) 9   C) 8.5
D) 9.5   E) 10

10) **O is the center of circle. CK=6cm, DK=?**

A) 2
B) 3
C) 4
D) 5
E) 6

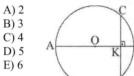

11) **KM=14cm, AO=OB, NL=?**

A) 6
B) 7
C) 8
D) 9
E) 14

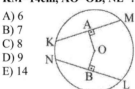

12) **O is the center of circle. AB=16cm, NO=OK, DC=?**

A) 16
B) 14
C) 12
D) 10
E) 6

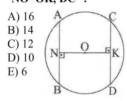

13) **O is the center of circle. $\angle A=90^o$, AB=12, AO=5, BK=?**

A) 6
B) 7
C) 8
D) 9
E) 10

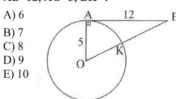

14) **$\angle A=90^o$, AO=10cm, $\dfrac{BK}{OK}=?$**

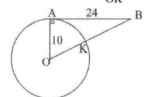

A) $\dfrac{10}{13}$ B) $\dfrac{13}{10}$ C) $\dfrac{12}{7}$

D) $\dfrac{7}{12}$ E) $\dfrac{8}{5}$

15) **$\angle A=90^o$, OC=4, BC=6, O is the center of circle. AB=?**

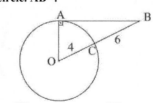

A) $2\sqrt{21}$ B) $3\sqrt{21}$
C) $2\sqrt{23}$ D) $\sqrt{85}$
E) $\sqrt{82}$

TEST – 28
(Inscribed Angles)

1) **O is the center of circle.** $\overset{\frown}{AB}$ **=80°, α=?**

   A) 80
   B) 60
   C) 50
   D) 40
   E) 30

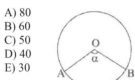

2) **∠D=120°, Find the ∠$\overset{\frown}{ABC}$ =?**

   A) 120
   B) 180
   C) 200
   D) 240
   E) 260

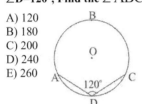

3) **It is given that ∠A=66°. What is ∠x=∠B=?**

   A) 22
   B) 33
   C) 44
   D) 66
   E) 88

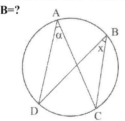

4) **∠$\overset{\frown}{ABC}$ =220°, α=?**

   A) 220
   B) 200
   C) 180
   D) 160
   E) 110

5) **∠x+∠α=?**

   A) 200
   B) 210
   C) 220
   D) 230
   E) 240

6) **∠D=40°, ∠B=36°, ∠C=y, ∠A=x, 2x+3y=?**

   A) 180
   B) 188
   C) 190
   D) 198
   E) 208

7) **∠$\overset{\frown}{AB}$ =110°, ∠DC=70°, α=?**

   A) 100
   B) 95
   C) 90
   D) 85
   E) 80

8) **$\overset{\frown}{AD}$ =177°, $\overset{\frown}{BD}$ =47°, ∠BCD=?**

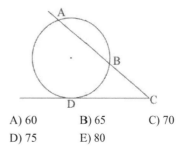

   A) 60   B) 65   C) 70
   D) 75   E) 80

9) $\angle \overset{\frown}{AC}$ =126º, ∠B=3x, x=?

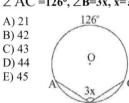

A) 21
B) 42
C) 43
D) 44
E) 45

10) $\angle \overset{\frown}{ADC}$ =122º, α=?

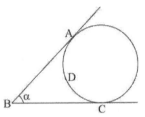

A) 50   B) 58   C) 48
D) 40   E) 36

11) $\angle \overset{\frown}{AE}$ =84º, $\angle \overset{\frown}{BD}$ =24º, ∠C=?

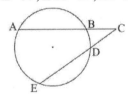

A) 24   B) 26   C) 30
D) 32   E) 60

12) **Find the value of x.**

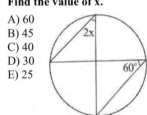

A) 60
B) 45
C) 40
D) 30
E) 25

13) $\angle \overset{\frown}{AB}$ =134º, $\angle \overset{\frown}{DC}$ =2x, ∠AKC=88º, x=?

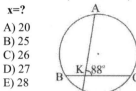

A) 20
B) 25
C) 26
D) 27
E) 28

14) $\angle \overset{\frown}{AB}$ =3x, $\angle \overset{\frown}{DC}$ =2x, ∠AOB=44º, x=?

A) $\dfrac{88}{7}$ B) $\dfrac{85}{2}$

C) $\dfrac{166}{5}$ D) $\dfrac{88}{5}$

E) 18

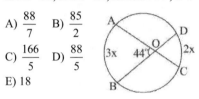

15) ∠A=54º, $\angle \overset{\frown}{BC}$ =2xº, $\angle \overset{\frown}{DE}$ =6xº, x=?

A) 54
B) 50
C) 48
D) 44
E) 27

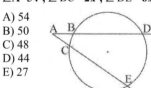

TEST – 29
(Segment Length in Circle)

1) Chords $\overline{AB}$ and $\overline{DC}$ intersect inside the circle. Find the value of x.

A) 1
B) 2
C) 3
D) 4
E) 5

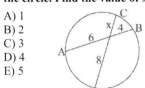

2) BC=4, BA=10, CD=6, DE=?

A) 2
B) 3
C) 4
D) 6
E) $\frac{10}{3}$

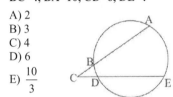

3) Find the value of x.

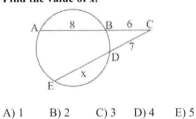

A) 1   B) 2   C) 3   D) 4   E) 5

4) AB=6, BC=5, x=?

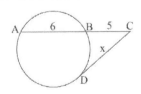

A) $\sqrt{44}$ B) $\sqrt{50}$ C) $\sqrt{55}$
D) $\pm\sqrt{66}$ E) ± 7

5) AD=8, BD=3, DC=7, ED=x=?

A) $\frac{46}{3}$
B) $\frac{56}{3}$
C) 21
D) 18
E) 17

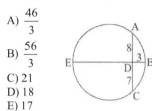

6) AB=6, BC=3, CD=?

A) 12
B) 11
C) 10
D) 9
E) 6

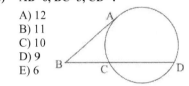

7) BC=x, CE=4x, DC=16, AC=5, x=?

A) $2\sqrt{3}$
B) $3\sqrt{3}$
C) $2\sqrt{5}$
D) $4\sqrt{5}$
E) $3\sqrt{7}$

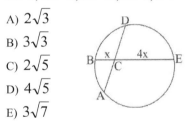

8) x=?

A) ±4
B) −4
C) 4
D) 6
E) ±6

9) AD=AE=2, BD=3x, EC=6, x=?

A) 1
B) 2
C) 3
D) 4
E) 6

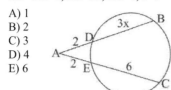

10) x=?

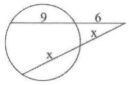

A) $3\sqrt{3}$ B) $2\sqrt{3}$ C) $-3\sqrt{3}$

D) $3\sqrt{5}$ E) $\sqrt{5}$

11) O is the center of circle. AB=8, BC=4, r=?

A) 2
B) 3
C) 4
D) 6
E) 8

12) BC=4, CO=3, AB=?

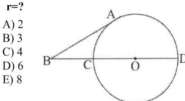

A) $\sqrt{10}$ B) $2\sqrt{10}$ C) $3\sqrt{10}$

D) $3\sqrt{5}$ E) $3\sqrt{6}$

13) x=?

A) 5
B) 6
C) 10
D) $2\sqrt{5}$
E) $2\sqrt{6}$

14) BC=3, DC=6, AB=?

A) $\sqrt{3}$
B) $\sqrt{6}$
C) $2\sqrt{2}$
D) $2\sqrt{3}$
E) $3\sqrt{3}$

15) CB=3, BA=6, CD=2, DE=x=?

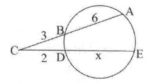

A) $\dfrac{23}{3}$ B) $\dfrac{23}{2}$ C) $\dfrac{24}{5}$

D) $\dfrac{25}{6}$ E) $\dfrac{27}{4}$

TEST – 30
(Circumference and Arc Length)

1) α=60°, r=6cm, find the length of the arc
AB=?

A) π   B) 2π

C) $\dfrac{3\pi}{2}$ D) 4π

E) $\dfrac{5\pi}{2}$

2) α=100°, r=3cm, find the length of the arc
AB=?

A) $\dfrac{4\pi}{3}$ B) $\dfrac{2\pi}{3}$

C) $\dfrac{3\pi}{2}$ D) $\dfrac{5\pi}{3}$

E) 3π

3) Find the circumference of a circle with
radius 5 inch.

A) 20π   B) 18π   C) 12π

D) 11π   E) 10π

4) Find the radius of a circle with
circumference 12π.

A) 2   B) 3   C) 4   D) 5   E) 6

5) ∠BOC=30°, AB=40cm, $\overset{\frown}{BC}$ = ?

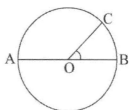

A) $\dfrac{10\pi}{3}$ B) $\dfrac{4\pi}{3}$ C) $\dfrac{5\pi}{2}$

D) $\dfrac{5\pi}{7}$ E) 2π

6) Find the diameter of a circle with
circumference $4\sqrt{3}\,\pi$.

A) $\sqrt{3}$ B) $2\sqrt{3}$ C) $3\sqrt{3}$

D) $4\sqrt{3}$ E) $8\sqrt{3}$

7) O is the center of circle. ∠AOB=140°,
BO=5cm. Find the length of arc

$\overset{\frown}{ACD}$ = ?

A) $\dfrac{25\pi}{4}$ B) $\dfrac{25\pi}{9}$ C) $\dfrac{35\pi}{7}$

D) $\dfrac{35\pi}{8}$ E) $\dfrac{35\pi}{9}$

8) AO=12cm, ∠AOB=20°, $\overset{\frown}{\angle AB} = ?$

A) $\dfrac{2\pi}{3}$ B) $\dfrac{3\pi}{2}$ C) $\dfrac{4\pi}{3}$

D) $\dfrac{3\pi}{4}$ E) 2π

9) Find the circumference of a circle with diameter $\sqrt{44}$cm. .

A) 2π B) 22π

C) $2\pi\sqrt{44}$ D) $11\pi\sqrt{2}$

E) $2\sqrt{11}\pi$

10) $\overline{AC} = (2y+20)°$, ∠ABC=(3x+30)°, x+y=?

A) 95
B) 100
C) 105
D) 110
E) 115

11) O is the center of circle. ∠AOB=120°, $\overline{AB} = 3x + 90^0$, x=?

A) 5
B) 10
C) 15
D) 20
E) 25

12) The radius of a circle is 13. Find the length of an arc of the circle intercepted by a central angle measuring 120°.

A) $\dfrac{11\pi}{3}$ B) $\dfrac{22\pi}{3}$ C) $\dfrac{24\pi}{5}$

D) $\dfrac{26\pi}{3}$ E) $\dfrac{256\pi}{3}$

13) AO=$\sqrt{3}$, ∠AOB=40°, Find the length of $\overset{\frown}{AB}$.

A) $\dfrac{2\sqrt{3}\pi}{9}$ B) $\dfrac{2\pi}{9}$

C) $\dfrac{2\sqrt{3}}{9}$ D) $\dfrac{3\sqrt{2}\pi}{9}$

E) $\dfrac{4\sqrt{2}\pi}{9}$

14) The radius of a circle is 18. Find the length of an arc of the circle intercepted by a central angle measuring 18°.

A) $\dfrac{9\pi}{2}$ B) $\dfrac{9\pi}{7}$ C) $\dfrac{9\pi}{5}$

D) $\dfrac{7\pi}{3}$ E) $\dfrac{7\pi}{5}$

15) Find the circumference of a circle with diameter $\sqrt{90}$ cm.

A) $3\sqrt{10}\pi$ B) $2\sqrt{10}\pi$

C) $\sqrt{10}\pi$ D) $2\pi\sqrt{10}$

E) $2\pi\sqrt{15}$

TEST – 31
(Areas of Circles and Sectors)

1) r=1.2cm, Find the area of the ○A.

A) 24π
B) 12π
C) 1.44π
D) 14.4π
E) 144π

2) A=196π, Find the radius of the ○B.

A) 10
B) 11
C) 12
D) 14
E) 28

3) A=289π, Find the diameter.

A) 36
B) 35
C) 34
D) 20
E) 17π

4) ∠AOB=75°, BO=6, Find the area of the sector shown at the right.

A) $\frac{12\pi}{5}$ B) $\frac{13\pi}{5}$

C) $\frac{15\pi}{7}$ D) $\frac{17\pi}{5}$

E) $\frac{15\pi}{2}$

5) ∠AOB=110°, r=18cm, Find the area of the sector shown at the right.

A) 99π
B) 88π
C) 77π
D) 66π
E) 44π

6) AO=12cm, $\angle ACB = 140°$ Find the area of the shaded region.

A) 14π
B) 18π
C) 20π
D) 36π
E) 56π

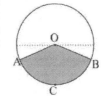

7) $AB = 4\sqrt{3}$ cm, Find the area of the shaded region.

A) 12π
B) 10π
C) 8π
D) 6π
E) $2\sqrt{3}\ \pi$

8) AO=6cm, AO=OB=AB. Find the area of the shaded region.

A) $7\pi - 7\sqrt{3}$

B) $8\pi - 8\sqrt{3}$

C) $6\pi - 9\sqrt{3}$

D) $6\pi + 9\sqrt{3}$

E) $12\pi - 9\sqrt{3}$

9) AO=6cm, ∠AOB=30°.
Find the area of the shaded region.

A) 11π
B) 22π
C) 33π
D) 44π
E) 66π

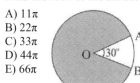

13) $AB = 4\sqrt{3}$, $DC = 4\sqrt{2}$. Find the ratio area of the shaded circles.

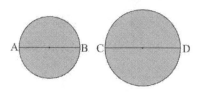

A) $\dfrac{1}{2}$ B) $\dfrac{1}{3}$ C) 3

D) $\dfrac{3}{2}$ E) $\dfrac{3}{4}$

10) AD=12, BC=6. Find the area of the shaded region.

A) 27π
B) 23π
C) 20π
D) 12π
E) 10π

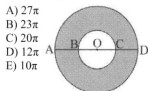

14) $AB = \sqrt{44}$. Find the area of the shaded region.

A) $\dfrac{11\pi}{2}$ B) 22π

C) $\sqrt{11}\pi$ D) $\sqrt{22}\pi$

E) $\sqrt{44}\pi$

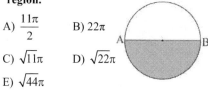

11) AB=BC=CD=DE=EF=FA=6,
Find the area of the shaded region.

A) $16\sqrt{3} - 2\pi$

B) $8\sqrt{3} - 2\pi$

C) $\dfrac{18\sqrt{3} - 9\pi}{2}$

D) $4\sqrt{3} - \pi$

E) $3\sqrt{3} + 2\pi$

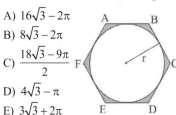

12) O is the center of the circle. AO=4cm, ∠AOB=108°. Find the area of the shaded region.

A) 6π B) 7π

C) $\dfrac{24\pi}{7}$ D) $\dfrac{24\pi}{5}$

E) 3π

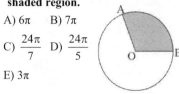

15) A and B are circle center. BC=2cm, Find the area of the shaded region.

A) 12π
B) 24π
C) 48π
D) 50π
E) 64π

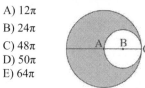

TEST – 32
(Surface Area of Prism and Cylinder)

1) Find the surface area of the right prism.

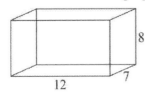

A) 170   B) 200   C) 250
D) 300   E) 472

2) Find the surface area of a rectangular prism.

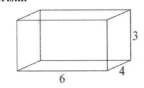

A) 80   B) 90   C) 100
D) 108   E) 180

3) Find the surface area.

A) 396
B) 386
C) 376
D) 366
E) 356

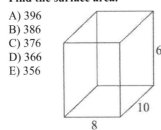

4) Find the surface area of a rectangular prism with sides of length 3,4 and 5cm.

A) 90   B) 94   C) 96
D) 98   E) 104

5) Find the surface area of a rectangular prism if the base is square with edge length 8cm and height 3cm.

A) 124
B) 144
C) 164
D) 184
E) 224

6) Find the surface of right rectangular prism with a height of 7cm, a length of 4cm and width of 6cm.

A) 148
B) 168
C) 178
D) 188
E) 208

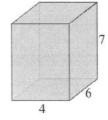

7) FC=12, DF=9, AD=13cm.
Find the surface area.

A) 576
B) 546
C) 476
D) 466
E) 356

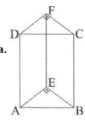

8) ∠E=∠F=90º, FA=5, BE=12, BC=8cm.
Find the prism side area.

A) 200
B) 220
C) 240
D) 260
E) 280

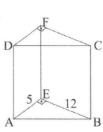

9) $\frac{1}{a} + \frac{1}{b} + \frac{1}{c} = 3$ and $\upsilon=144cm^3$, Find the surface area of rectangular prism.

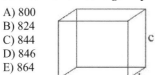

A) 800
B) 824
C) 844
D) 846
E) 864

10) KL=5cm, LD=4cm. Find the surface area of the right cylinder.

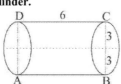

A) 40π
B) 50π
C) 62π
D) 72π
E) 84π

11) AB=6cm, r=3cm. Find the surface area of the cylinder.

A) 54π B) 54   C) 44π
D) 44   E) 34π

12) BC=11cm, AB=12cm. Find the surface area of the cylinder.

A) 200
B) 214π
C) 204π
D) 206π
E) 224

13) AB=6x, BC=2x. Find the surface area of the cylinder.

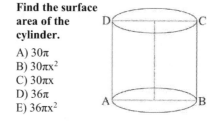

A) 30π
B) $30\pi x^2$
C) $30\pi x$
D) 36π
E) $36\pi x^2$

14) ABCD is cylinder. $\frac{r}{h} = \frac{1}{3}$. Find the surface area of cylinder.

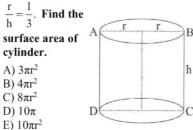

A) $3\pi r^2$
B) $4\pi r^2$
C) $8\pi r^2$
D) 10π
E) $10\pi r^2$

15) AB=3^{2x}, BC=3^x. Find the surface area of cylinder.

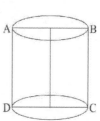

A) $3^{3x}\pi + 2 \cdot 3^{4x}\pi$
B) $\frac{3^{4x} \cdot \pi}{2} + 3^{3x}\pi$
C) $3^{3x}\pi + 3^{4x}$
D) $\frac{3^{4x} \cdot \pi}{3} + 3^{3x} + \pi$
E) $3^{3x}\pi + 4 \cdot 3^{2x}\pi$

TEST – 33
(Surface Area of Pyramids and Cones)

1) Find the surface of a triangular pyramid if the area of its base is 16cm² and each of its literal face has area 9cm².

A) 43   B) 44   C) 46   D) 47   E) 48

2) Find the base area of a square pyramid whose base has a side length of 12cm.

A) 148   B) 144   C) 143
D) 140   E) 121

3) The base area of a square pyramid is 225cm². Find the length of an edge of the base of the pyramid.

A) 12   B) 13   C) 14   D) 15   E) 16

4) This diagram shows a square–based pyramid with base length 16 in and height 6cm. What is the base area of the square–based pyramid?

A) 126
B) 132
C) 220
D) 256
E) 264

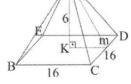

5) What is the surface area of the pyramid?

A) 426   B) 526   C) 576
D) 580   E) 600

6) EK=8, AB=6. Find the surface area of the regular pyramid shown.

A) 96
B) 102
C) 122
D) 130
E) 132

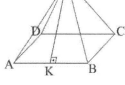

7) AB=4, EK=5. AB=BC. Find the surface area of the regular pyramid.

A) 48
B) 50
C) 54
D) 52
E) 56

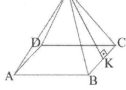

8) AB=BC=9, EK=12. Find the surface area of the regular pyramid shown.

A) 280
B) 282
C) 297
D) 300
E) 312

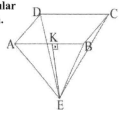

9) Find the surface area of the right cone shown.

A) 48π
B) 49π
C) 50π
D) 51π
E) 60π

13) AK=16, KC=12. Find the surface area of the right cone.

A) 360π
B) 384π
C) 390π
D) 400π
E) 420π

10) AC=13, BC=10cm. Find the surface area of the right cone.

A) 90
B) 80π
C) 90π
D) 100π
E) 121π

14) KC=4, AK=6. Find the surface area of the right cone.

A) $16\pi + 8\sqrt{13}\pi$
B) $14\pi + 8\sqrt{13}\pi$
C) $17\pi + 6\sqrt{13}\pi$
D) $12\pi + 4\sqrt{13}\pi$
E) 20π

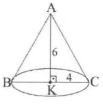

11) AB=16, AC=12. Find the surface area of the right cone.

A) 132π
B) 132
C) 144π
D) 144
E) 256π

12) AB=24cm, CK=5cm, Find the slant height of the right cone.

A) 10
B) 11
C) 12
D) 13
E) 14

15) DC=10, AD=12. Find the slant height of the right cone.

A) $\sqrt{61}$
B) $2\sqrt{61}$
C) $\sqrt{71}$
D) $2\sqrt{71}$
E) 18

TEST – 34
(Volume of Prisms and Cylinders)

1) a=6cm. Find the prisms volume.

A) 36
B) 108
C) 124
D) 216
E) 230

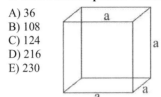

2) Find the prisms volume.

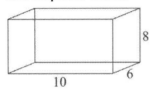

A) 430   B) 480   C) 490
D) 512   E) 480π

3) υ=120cm³. Find the x.

A) 6
B) 7
C) 8
D) 9
E) 10

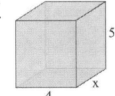

4) What is the volume of a prism where the base area is 36cm² and which is 13cm long?

A) 458   B) 468   C) 478
D) 512   E) 578

5) υ=64cm³. 2x=?

A) 2
B) 4
C) 5
D) 6
E) 7

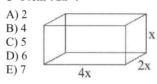

6) Find the volume of the right prisms.

A) 123
B) 243
C) 333
D) 343
E) 363

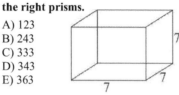

7) Find the volume of the right prism.

A) 90
B) 120
C) 220
D) 320
E) 420

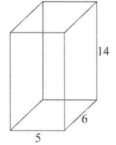

8) Find the ratio volume (V₁:V₂).

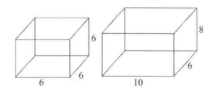

A) $\frac{9}{22}$ B) $\frac{9}{20}$ C) $\frac{7}{20}$

D) $\frac{8}{21}$ E) $\frac{10}{21}$

9) r=4cm, h=8cm. Find the volume of the right cylinder.

A) 100π
B) 112π
C) 128π
D) 130π
E) 168π

10) r=4cm, h=4cm. Find the volume of the right cylinder.

A) 64π
B) 64
C) 100π
D) 100
E) 32π

11) AB=4cm, BD=12cm. Find the volume of the right cylinder.

A) 40π
B) 48π
C) 50π
D) 50π
E) 64π

12) r=6cm, AB=10cm. Find the volume of the oblique cylinder.

A) 100π
B) 120π
C) 180π
D) 360π
E) 380π

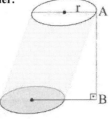

13) AB=3cm, AD=14cm. Find the volume of the right cylinder.

A) 80π
B) 90π
C) 90
D) 120π
E) 126π

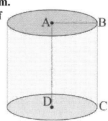

14) AB=8cm, BC=18cm. Find the volume of the oblique cylinder.

A) 1152
B) 1152π
C) 1262π
D) 1262
E) 166π

15) AB=20cm, BC=12cm. EF=12cm, KF=10cm. $(V_1:V_2)$=?

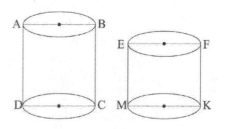

A) $\dfrac{10}{3}$
B) $\dfrac{10}{7}$
C) $\dfrac{11}{3}$
D) $\dfrac{11}{7}$
E) 2

TEST – 35
(Volume of Pyramids and Cones)

1) EK=20, AB=12. Find the volume of the pyramid with the square base shown the right.

A) 860
B) 960
C) 980
D) 1000
E) 1200

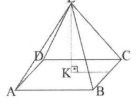

2) AB=BC=14cm, EK=16cm. Find the volume of the pyramid.

A) 1000.3
B) 1015.3
C) 1045.3
D) 1060.3
E) 1080.3

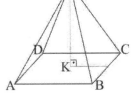

3) ∠B=90°, AB=9, BC=12, h=16. Find the volume of the pyramid.

A) 158
B) 168
C) 178
D) 288
E) 208

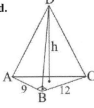

4) AB=BC=AC=6cm, h=8cm. Find the volume of the pyramid.

A) $12\sqrt{3}$
B) $14\sqrt{3}$
C) $16\sqrt{3}$
D) $20\sqrt{3}$
E) $24\sqrt{3}$

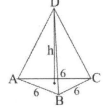

5) ABCD is square. EK=14cm, AB=12cm. Find the volume of the pyramid.

A) 672
B) 675
C) 682
D) 782
E) 800

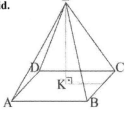

6) AB=BC=CD=DE=EF=FA=10cm, h=18cm. Find the volume of the pyramid.

A) $500\sqrt{3}$
B) $600\sqrt{3}$
C) $700\sqrt{3}$
D) $900\sqrt{3}$
E) 1200

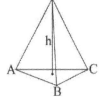

7) AB=BC=AC=15cm, h=21cm. Find the volume of the pyramid.

A) $320\sqrt{3}$
B) $340\sqrt{3}$
C) $394\sqrt{3}$
D) 394
E) $396\sqrt{2}$

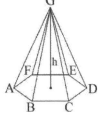

8) AB=BC=20cm, EK=22cm. Find the volume of the pyramid.

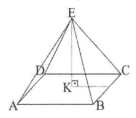

A) $\dfrac{7700}{4}$
B) $\dfrac{8800}{3}$
C) $\dfrac{9400}{3}$
D) 3000
E) 2500

9) ABC is the right circular cone. KC=6cm, AK=10cm. Find the volume of the cone.

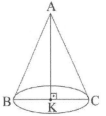

A) 110π B) 120π
C) 130π D) 140π
E) 150π

10) r=5cm, h=8cm, Find the volume of the cone.

A) $\dfrac{200}{3}$

B) $\dfrac{200\pi}{3}$

C) $\dfrac{400}{3}$

D) $\dfrac{400\pi}{3}$

E) 60π

11) DC=7cm, AD=10cm. Find the volume of the cone.

A) 490π

B) $\dfrac{490\pi}{3}$

C) $\dfrac{409\pi}{3}$

D) 160
E) 180

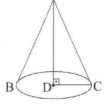

12) DC=6cm. V=120πcm³, h=?

A) 10
B) 11
C) 12
D) 13
E) 16

13) AD=8cm, V=128π. DC=r=?

A) $2\sqrt{3}$

B) $3\sqrt{3}$

C) $4\sqrt{3}$

D) $4\sqrt{2}$

E) $4\sqrt{5}$

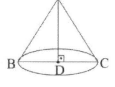

14) BD=2x, AD=3x, Find the volume of the cone.

A) $4x^3$
B) $4x^2$
C) $5x^3\pi$
D) $\pi4x^3$
E) $6x^3\pi$

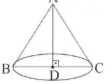

15) DC $=\sqrt{5}$cm, AD $=\sqrt{7}$cm.. Find the volume of the cone.

A) $\dfrac{5\pi}{3}$

B) $\dfrac{7\pi}{3}$

C) $\dfrac{5\pi\sqrt{3}}{3}$

D) $\dfrac{7\pi\sqrt{5}}{4}$

E) $\dfrac{5\sqrt{7}\pi}{3}$

TEST – 36
(Surface Area and Volume of Spheres)

1) OA=r=11cm. Find the surface area of sphere.

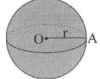

A) 22π
B) 33π
C) 88π
D) 121
E) 484π

2) OA=13cm. Find the surface area of sphere.

A) 169π
B) 149π
C) 121π
D) 100π
E) 676π

3) OA=r=12.2cm. Find the surface area of sphere.

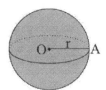

A) 595.36
B) 595.36π
C) 605.35π
D) 614.68π
E) 620

4) AB=14cm. Find the surface area of sphere.

A) 196
B) 196π
C) 49π
D) 49
E) 89π

5) AB=12.6cm. Find the surface area of sphere.

A) 158.76π
B) 148.76π
C) 160
D) 164π
E) 458

6) The area of sphere $400\pi cm^2$. Find the radius.

A) 4   B) 5   C) 6   D) 7   E) 10

7) The sphere radius is $3\pi cm$. Find the area of sphere.

A) 36   B) 36π C) $36\pi^3$
D) 72π E) $72\pi^3$

8) OA=4cm. Find the volume of sphere. (π=3.14)

A) 268
B) 270
C) 280
D) 290
E) 300

9) OA=3.3cm. Find the volume of sphere. (π=3.14)

A) 150.53
B) 155.12
C) 160.53
D) 165.43
E) 170.12

13) AB=6cm, DC=4cm. Find the ratio of volume spheres (V_1:V_2).

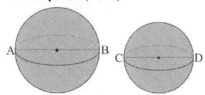

A) $\dfrac{27}{8}$ B) $\dfrac{27}{7}$ C) $\dfrac{28}{7}$

D) $\dfrac{28}{9}$ E) 4

10) AB=20cm. Find the volume of the sphere. (π=3.14)

A) 4167
B) 4187
C) 4287
D) 4444
E) 4560

11) The volume of sphere is 200πcm³. Find the sphere radius.

A) 5   B) $5\sqrt{2}$ C) $5\sqrt{3}$

D) $4\sqrt{2}$ E) $4\sqrt{3}$

14) OA=r=2.2cm. Find the volume of the sphere. (π=3.14)

A) 22.3
B) 33.3
C) 44.6
D) 55.6
E) 66.6

12) Find the sphere volume of radius is 2πcm.

A) $32\pi^2$ B) $32\pi^3$ C) $32\pi^4$

D) $\dfrac{32\pi^4}{3}$ E) 64π

15) The sphere volume is 160πcm³. Find the sphere radius.

A) $2\sqrt{15}$ B) $2\sqrt[3]{15}$ C) $3\sqrt{15}$

D) $3\sqrt[3]{15}$ E) $4\sqrt{15}$

TEST – 37
(Matrix)

1) $A=\begin{bmatrix}4&3\\2&1\end{bmatrix}$, $B=\begin{bmatrix}4&5\\3&6\end{bmatrix}$, $A+B=?$

A) $\begin{bmatrix}8&8\\5&7\end{bmatrix}$ 　 B) $\begin{bmatrix}8&8\\6&7\end{bmatrix}$

C) $\begin{bmatrix}6&7\\8&9\end{bmatrix}$ 　 D) $\begin{bmatrix}7&7\\3&6\end{bmatrix}$

E) $\begin{bmatrix}6&8\\10&11\end{bmatrix}$

2) $A=\begin{bmatrix}9&11\\7&3\end{bmatrix}$, $B=\begin{bmatrix}6&4\\3&2\end{bmatrix}$, $A-B=?$

A) $\begin{bmatrix}3&4\\4&1\end{bmatrix}$ 　 B) $\begin{bmatrix}3&7\\4&1\end{bmatrix}$

C) $\begin{bmatrix}3&7\\1&4\end{bmatrix}$ 　 D) $\begin{bmatrix}6&6\\3&2\end{bmatrix}$

E) $\begin{bmatrix}6&4\\3&3\end{bmatrix}$

3) $A=\begin{bmatrix}4&3\\2&7\end{bmatrix}$, $3A=?$

A) $\begin{bmatrix}4&3\\2&7\end{bmatrix}$ 　 B) $\begin{bmatrix}8&6\\4&14\end{bmatrix}$

C) $\begin{bmatrix}12&9\\4&21\end{bmatrix}$ 　 D) $\begin{bmatrix}12&9\\6&21\end{bmatrix}$

E) $\begin{bmatrix}12&9\\6&12\end{bmatrix}$

4) $A=\begin{bmatrix}6&4\\3&2\end{bmatrix}$, $B=\begin{bmatrix}2&3\\1&2\end{bmatrix}$, $3A-2B=?$

A) $\begin{bmatrix}14&5\\8&4\end{bmatrix}$ 　 B) $\begin{bmatrix}14&6\\7&4\end{bmatrix}$

C) $\begin{bmatrix}14&6\\8&2\end{bmatrix}$ 　 D) $\begin{bmatrix}13&6\\8&4\end{bmatrix}$

E) $\begin{bmatrix}6&12\\7&3\end{bmatrix}$

5) $A=\begin{bmatrix}6&4\\8&12\end{bmatrix}$, $B=\begin{bmatrix}8&10\\6&4\end{bmatrix}$,

$A+B=\begin{bmatrix}14&2x\\14&4y\end{bmatrix}$, **x+y=?**

A) 11　B) 12　C) 13　D) 14　E) 15

6) $A=\begin{bmatrix}14&12\\20&16\end{bmatrix}$, $B=\begin{bmatrix}4&4\\6&6\end{bmatrix}$

$A-B=\begin{bmatrix}5x&8\\7y&10\end{bmatrix}$, **2x+3y=?**

A) 10　B) 11　C) 12　D) 13　E) 14

7) $A = \begin{bmatrix} 0 & 1 \\ 3 & 4 \end{bmatrix}$, $B = \begin{bmatrix} 4 & 3 \\ 2 & 1 \end{bmatrix}$, $A + B = ?$

A) $\begin{bmatrix} 5 & 4 \\ 6 & 5 \end{bmatrix}$ B) $\begin{bmatrix} 4 & 4 \\ 5 & 5 \end{bmatrix}$

C) $\begin{bmatrix} 3 & 4 \\ 5 & 5 \end{bmatrix}$ D) $\begin{bmatrix} 6 & 4 \\ 2 & 2 \end{bmatrix}$

E) $\begin{bmatrix} 0 & 4 \\ 3 & 7 \end{bmatrix}$

8) $A = \begin{bmatrix} 1 & 2 \\ 3 & 4 \end{bmatrix}$, $B = \begin{bmatrix} 0 & 2 \\ 1 & 3 \end{bmatrix}$. **Find the AB matrix.**

A) $\begin{bmatrix} 3 & 8 \\ 4 & 14 \end{bmatrix}$ B) $\begin{bmatrix} 3 & 8 \\ 14 & 4 \end{bmatrix}$

C) $\begin{bmatrix} 7 & 3 \\ 2 & 1 \end{bmatrix}$ D) $\begin{bmatrix} 3 & 8 \\ 4 & 6 \end{bmatrix}$

E) $\begin{bmatrix} 2 & 8 \\ 4 & 18 \end{bmatrix}$

9) $A = \begin{bmatrix} 1 & 2 & 3 \\ 4 & 6 & 7 \end{bmatrix}$, **Find the scalar factor 2.**

A) $\begin{bmatrix} 1 & 2 & 6 \\ 8 & 12 & 14 \end{bmatrix}$ B) $\begin{bmatrix} 2 & 4 & 6 \\ 8 & 12 & 14 \end{bmatrix}$

C) $\begin{bmatrix} 2 & 4 & 6 \\ 9 & 12 & 14 \end{bmatrix}$ D) $\begin{bmatrix} 7 & 3 & 2 \\ 4 & 8 & 10 \end{bmatrix}$

E) $\begin{bmatrix} 1 & 4 & 12 \\ 8 & 12 & 14 \end{bmatrix}$

10) $A = \begin{bmatrix} 7 & 5 & 25 \\ 2 & -10 & 9 \end{bmatrix}$, **Find the A matrix transpose.**

A) $\begin{bmatrix} 7 & 2 \\ 5 & 9 \\ 25 & 10 \end{bmatrix}$ B) $\begin{bmatrix} 7 & 2 \\ 5 & -10 \\ 25 & 9 \end{bmatrix}$

C) $\begin{bmatrix} 7 & 2 \\ 5 & -10 \\ 2 & 9 \end{bmatrix}$ D) $\begin{bmatrix} 7 & 9 \\ 5 & -10 \\ 25 & 2 \end{bmatrix}$

E) $\begin{bmatrix} 6 & 2 \\ 4 & 1 \\ 3 & 7 \end{bmatrix}$

11) **What is the transpose of the matrix** $\begin{bmatrix} 1 & 2 & 4 \\ 8 & 9 & 10 \end{bmatrix}$?

A) $\begin{bmatrix} 1 & 8 \\ 2 & 9 \\ 4 & 10 \end{bmatrix}$ B) $\begin{bmatrix} 1 & 8 \\ 4 & 9 \\ 2 & 10 \end{bmatrix}$ C) $\begin{bmatrix} 1 & 10 \\ 2 & 9 \\ 4 & 8 \end{bmatrix}$

D) $\begin{bmatrix} 1 & 9 \\ 2 & 9 \\ 4 & 10 \end{bmatrix}$ E) $\begin{bmatrix} 8 & 9 & 10 \\ 1 & 2 & 4 \end{bmatrix}$

12) **What is the transpose of the matrix** $\begin{bmatrix} 2 & 4 & 6 \\ 8 & 9 & 10 \\ 11 & 12 & 3 \end{bmatrix}$?

A) $\begin{bmatrix} 2 & 8 & 11 \\ 4 & 9 & 12 \\ 6 & 10 & 13 \end{bmatrix}$ B) $\begin{bmatrix} 2 & 8 & 11 \\ 4 & 9 & 12 \\ 6 & 10 & 3 \end{bmatrix}$

C) $\begin{bmatrix} 2 & 4 & 6 \\ 4 & 9 & 10 \\ 12 & 11 & 3 \end{bmatrix}$ D) $\begin{bmatrix} 2 & 8 & 13 \\ 4 & 9 & 12 \\ 6 & 10 & 11 \end{bmatrix}$

E) $\begin{bmatrix} 2 & 6 & 4 \\ 4 & 10 & 9 \\ 6 & 3 & 12 \end{bmatrix}$

13) $A = \begin{bmatrix} 1 & 2 \\ 3 & 4 \end{bmatrix}$, $B = \begin{bmatrix} 5 & 6 \\ 7 & 8 \end{bmatrix}$, then what is $A+B^T$?

A) $\begin{bmatrix} 6 & 9 \\ 12 & 9 \end{bmatrix}$ B) $\begin{bmatrix} 6 & 8 \\ 9 & 12 \end{bmatrix}$

C) $\begin{bmatrix} 6 & 9 \\ 9 & 12 \end{bmatrix}$ D) $\begin{bmatrix} 6 & 7 \\ 8 & 9 \end{bmatrix}$

E) $\begin{bmatrix} 3 & 4 \\ 7 & 8 \end{bmatrix}$

14) $A = \begin{bmatrix} 1 & 2 & 3 \\ -2 & 3 & 4 \end{bmatrix}$, $B = \begin{bmatrix} -2 & 4 & 3 \\ 2 & 0 & 1 \end{bmatrix}$, then, what is $3A+2B=$?

A) $\begin{bmatrix} -1 & 14 & 15 \\ -2 & 9 & 14 \end{bmatrix}$ B) $\begin{bmatrix} -1 & 14 & 15 \\ 14 & 9 & -2 \end{bmatrix}$

C) $\begin{bmatrix} -1 & 14 & 15 \\ 11 & 12 & 3 \end{bmatrix}$ D) $\begin{bmatrix} 15 & 14 & -1 \\ -2 & 9 & 1 \end{bmatrix}$

E) $\begin{bmatrix} 3 & 4 & 5 \\ 6 & 7 & 8 \end{bmatrix}$

15) $A = \begin{bmatrix} 1 & 2 \\ 3 & 4 \end{bmatrix}$, $B = \begin{bmatrix} 5 & 6 \\ 7 & 8 \end{bmatrix}$, then what is $2A^T+3B^T$?

A) $\begin{bmatrix} 17 & 27 \\ 0 & 4 \end{bmatrix}$ B) $\begin{bmatrix} 17 & 27 \\ 22 & 32 \end{bmatrix}$

C) $\begin{bmatrix} 17 & 27 \\ 22 & 23 \end{bmatrix}$ D) $\begin{bmatrix} 17 & 17 \\ 0 & 4 \end{bmatrix}$

E) $\begin{bmatrix} 16 & 17 & 27 \\ 4 & 3 & 2 \end{bmatrix}$

TEST– 1
(*Solutions*)

1) $\angle ACD+\angle DCE+\angle ECA=180°$,
   $70°+\angle DCE+44°=180°$,
   $\angle DCE=66°$

2) $2x+2x+2x+3x=180°$,
   $9x=180°$,
   $x=20°$

3) $\angle ABD-\angle LBD=24°$
   $\angle ABD+\angle LBD=180°$
   $+\underline{}$ Instead of L--C
   $2\angle ABD=204°$
   $\angle ABD=102°$

4) $\angle ABD=\angle DBC=34°$,
   $\angle ABC=34+34=68°$

5) $\angle ABD=\angle DBC=44°$

6) $\angle ABD+\angle DBC=90°$,
   $\angle ABD+27°=90°$,
   $\angle ABD=63°$

7) $\dfrac{\angle ABD}{\angle DBC}=\dfrac{1}{3}=\dfrac{x}{3x}$
   $x+3x=90° \Rightarrow 4x=90°$, $x=22,5°$
   $\angle DBL=3x=3\cdot22,5=67,5°$

------question and solution don't match.

8) $\angle ABD=\angle DBC$,
   $8x=7x+8 \Rightarrow x=8°$

9) $\angle ABD=\angle CBD$

   $8x-20=3x+30$
   $5x=50$
   $x=10$
   $\angle ABC=11x+10=11x10+10=120$

10) $\angle ACE+\angle ECD=90°$,
    $4x+x=90°$, $x=18°$

11) $x+y=180°$, $x=64°$,
    $2x+y=x+x+y=64°+180°=244°$

12) $4x=144$,
    $x=36°$

13) $3x+100=124$,
    $3x=24$,
    $x=8°$

14) $\angle ABD=\angle EBL$
    $82=4x+2$,
    $80=4x$,
    $x=20°$

15) $\angle A+\angle B=90°$,
    $4x+4+x+1=90$
    $5x+5=90$
    $5x=85$, $x=17°$,
    $\angle A=4x+4=4\cdot17+4=72$

TEST– 2
(*Solutions*)

1) $130°+(x+20°)=180°$,
$x+150°=180°$, $x=30°$

2) $3x+45°=180°$,
$3x=135°$,
$x=45°$

3) $103°=3x-14$,
$117°=3x$, $x=39°$

4) $x=44°$, $y=44°$,
$2x-y=2\cdot44°-44°=44°$

5) $\angle x=82°$,
$x+y=180°$, $82+y=180$, $y=98$
$y-x=98-82=16$

6) $\angle ABD+\angle DBC=90°$,
$3x+3y=90°$,
$x+y=30°$

7) $2t+4y+2x=180°$
$t+2y+x=90°$

8) $x=88°$,
$2y+88°=180°$, $2y=92$, $y=46°$
$x+y=88+46=134$

9) $4y=130°$, $2x+4y=180°$
$2y=65°$ `x+2y=90°`

10) $100°=4x$, $x=25°$

11) $52°+\alpha+44°=180°$,
$\alpha=84°$,
$x+y+\alpha=180°$,
$x+y+84=180°$,
$x+y=96°$

12) $m+144°=180°$; $n+132°=180°$;
$m=36°$; $n=48°$;
$m+n+x=180°$,
$36°+48°+x=180°$,
$x=96°$

13) $154°+2y=180°$, $2x+146°=180°$
$2y=36°$ $2x=34°$
$y=18°$ $x=17°$
$3x+3y=3(x+y)=3(18+17)=3\cdot35=105$

14) $x+130°+120°=360°$,
$x+250°=360°$,
$x=110°$

15) $3x+3y+3t=360°$,
$3(x+y+t)=360°$,
$x+y+t=120°$

TEST– 3
(*Solutions*)

1) Slope$=\dfrac{y_2-y_1}{x_2-x_1}=\dfrac{4-8}{6-0}=\dfrac{-4}{6}=-\dfrac{2}{3}$

6) $A(x_1, y_1)=(8, 9)$, $x_1=8$, $y_1=9$,
Slope$=m=3$,
$y-y_1=m(x-x_1)$,
$y-9=3(x-8)$,
$y-9=3x-24 \Rightarrow y=3x-15$

2) Slope$=\dfrac{y_2-y_1}{x_2-x_1}=\dfrac{8-4}{-4-6}=\dfrac{4}{-10}=-\dfrac{2}{5}$

7) Slope$=m_1=-2$,
$m_1\|m_2$ if $m_2=-2$
$y-y_1=m(x-x_1)$,
$y-6=-2(x-2)$,
$y-6=-2x+4$,
$y=-2x+10$

3) Slope$=\dfrac{y_2-y_1}{x_2-x_1}=\dfrac{\sqrt{27}-2\sqrt{3}}{2\sqrt{2}-\sqrt{2}}$
$=\dfrac{3\sqrt{3}-2\sqrt{3}}{\sqrt{2}}=\dfrac{\sqrt{3}}{\sqrt{2}}$

8) $m_1\|m_2$ if Slope $m_1=$Slope m_2
$m_1=$slope$=\sqrt{3}$
$y-y_1=m(x-x_1)$,
$y-2\sqrt{3}=\sqrt{3}\ (x-\sqrt{3}\ )$,
$y-2\sqrt{3}=x\sqrt{3}-3$,
$y=x\sqrt{3}+2\sqrt{3}-3$

4) Slope$=\dfrac{y_2-y_1}{x_2-x_1}=\dfrac{8-10}{8-12}=\dfrac{-2}{-4}=\dfrac{1}{2}$

9) Slope$=3$

We can change question like "Find slope of the given equation."

5) $y-y_1=m(x-x_1)$,
$m=6$, $(x_1, y_1)=(3, 4)$
$y-4=6(x-3)$
$y-4=6x-18$
$y=6x-14$

10) $2x+7y+21=0$, $7y=-2x-21$,
Slope$=-\dfrac{2}{7}$

11) $y = \sqrt{3}\, x + 3\sqrt{3}$, Slope $= \sqrt{3}$

12) Slope $= \dfrac{3}{2}$

Slope $m_1 \cdot$ Slope $m_2 = -1$

$\dfrac{3}{2} \cdot$ Slope $m_2 = -1$, $\quad m_2 = -\dfrac{2}{3}$

$y - y_1 = m(x - x_1)$,

$y + 2 = -\dfrac{2}{3}(x - 4)$,

$y - 2\sqrt{3} = x\sqrt{3} - 3$,

$y = -\dfrac{2x}{3} + \dfrac{8}{3} + 2 \;\Rightarrow\; y = -\dfrac{2x}{3} + \dfrac{14}{3}$

13) Slope $m_1 \cdot$ Slope $m_2 = -1$,

$7 \cdot a = -1 \;\Rightarrow\; a = -\dfrac{1}{7}$

14) Slope $= 4$, $A(0, 6)$

$y - y_1 = m(x - x_1)$,

$y - 6 = 4(x - 0) \;\Rightarrow\; y = 4x + 6$

15) Slope $m_1 = \dfrac{2}{3}$, Slope $m_2 = \dfrac{3}{5}$

Sum $= \dfrac{2}{3} + \dfrac{3}{5} = \dfrac{10 + 9}{15} = \dfrac{19}{15}$

TEST– 4
(*Solutions*)

1) $y=ax+b$, slope=a
$y=4x+12$, slope=4

2) $ax+by+c=0$, slope=$-\dfrac{a}{b}$

$3x+6y+18=0$, slope=$-\dfrac{3}{6}=-\dfrac{1}{2}$

3) $y=\sqrt{3}x+3\sqrt{3}$,
slope=$\sqrt{3}$

4) $\sqrt{2}x+\sqrt{3}y+6=0$,
slope=$-\dfrac{\sqrt{2}}{\sqrt{3}}$

5) $y=4x+4$, slope=4

6) slope $m_1=-\dfrac{2}{3}$,

slope $m_2=-\dfrac{a}{4}$

$m_1\|m_2$, slope m_1=slope m_2,

$\left(+\dfrac{2}{3}\right)=-\dfrac{a}{4}$, $a=\dfrac{-8}{3}$

7) slope $m_1\cdot$ slope $m_2=-1$,
$-\dfrac{7}{6}\cdot\left(-\dfrac{a}{4}\right)=-1, 7a=-24, a=-\dfrac{24}{7}$
Answers should be – 24/7.

8) $\dfrac{x}{a}+\dfrac{y}{b}=1$, $\dfrac{x}{2}+\dfrac{y}{4}=1$, $2x+y=4$

9) $\dfrac{x}{a}+\dfrac{y}{b}=1$, $x=y=7$

$\dfrac{x}{7}+\dfrac{y}{7}=1$, $x+y=7$

10) slope=$\dfrac{y_2-y_1}{x_2-x_1}=\dfrac{13-4}{9-3}=\dfrac{9}{6}=\dfrac{3}{2}$

11) slope=$\dfrac{y_2-y_1}{x_2-x_1}=\dfrac{\sqrt{75}-2\sqrt{3}}{\sqrt{20}-\sqrt{5}}$

$=\dfrac{5\sqrt{3}-2\sqrt{3}}{2\sqrt{5}-\sqrt{5}}$

slope=$\dfrac{3\sqrt{3}}{\sqrt{5}}$

12) slope=$\dfrac{y_2-y_1}{x_2-x_1}=\dfrac{\dfrac{1}{3}-\dfrac{1}{6}}{\dfrac{1}{2}-\dfrac{1}{4}}=\dfrac{\dfrac{2-1}{6}}{\dfrac{2-1}{4}}$

$=\dfrac{\dfrac{1}{6}}{\dfrac{1}{4}}=\dfrac{4}{6}=\dfrac{2}{3}$

13) $\dfrac{3y}{2}=-\dfrac{2x}{3}-6$,

slope=$-\dfrac{-\dfrac{2}{3}}{\dfrac{3}{2}}=-\dfrac{4}{9}$

14) $\dfrac{x}{a}+\dfrac{y}{b}=1$, $\dfrac{x}{-6}+\dfrac{y}{-6}=1$, $x+y=-6$

15) $d_1=\dfrac{x}{a}+\dfrac{y}{b}=1$, $\dfrac{x}{4}+\dfrac{y}{-6}=1$

555 Questions and Solutions

TEST– 5
(*Solutions*)

1) AB=AC if ∠B=∠C=x
∠A+∠B+∠C=180°,
54+x+x=180°, 2x=126°, x=63°

2) ∠ACD=∠A+∠B,
110°=60°+x,
x=50°

3) ∠ACD=48°+90°,
3x=138°, x=46°

4) ∠A+∠B+∠C=180°,
2x+3x+90°=180°,
5x=90°, x=18°
4x=4·18°=72°

5) AB=BC=2x,
∠A+∠B+∠C=180°,
2x+90°+2x=180°,
4x=90°, x=22,5°,
4x=4·22,5°=90°

We don't need to find x.So we should cancel last part of solution.

6) AB=AC, ∠B=∠C=x,
∠A+∠B+∠C=180°,
122+x+x=180°,
2x=58°, x=29°

7) ∠A>∠B>∠C,
|BC|>|AC|>AB

We can add question: "Which of the following is correct for given triangle "or other version.

8) x+128°+124°=360°,

9) x=108°
3x+3x+3x=360°, 9x=360°, x=40°,
y+3x=180°, y+3·40°=180°, y=60°,
2x+3y=2·40+3·60=80+180=260°

10) 80+x=α

11) ∠DAC=∠ACD=2x,
∠DAB=∠ADC=y
∠ACD=2y, ∠ADB=4x
4x+2y=180,
y+2x=90°

12) ∠DAC=∠ADC=α, ∠ADB=2α,
∠ABD=∠ACD=α
∠B=∠C=α
α+2α+x=180°, x=180°–3α

13) ∠DAC+∠ACD+∠D=180°,
64°+∠ACD+90°=180°,
∠ACD=26°, ∠DCE=64°,
∠ECD+∠DCE=α=180°,
90°+64°+α=180°, α=26°,

14) AB=AC= angle B= angle C=a, ∠DBC=a–m,
∠ADB=2a–m,
m+x+2a–m=180°, a=180–x, 3a=540–3x

15) AB=BC=AC, ∠B=∠A=∠C=60°,
AC=DC, ∠CAD=∠ACD=2x,
2x=60°, x=30°, x²=900

87

It will be better to draw a picture for the solt.

TEST– 6
(*Solutions*)

1) $12=4x$, $x=3$

2) $4y-5=23$, $4y=28$, $y=7^\circ$

3) $AE=FL$, $4x+4=12$, $4x=8$, $x=2$

4) $\angle D=42^\circ$, $\angle K=5y-8$, $5y-8=42^\circ$,
     $5y=50$, $y=10^\circ$

5) $x=66^\circ$

6) $\angle F=\angle C$, $64=3x+4$, $60=3x$, $x=20^\circ$

7) $\angle A+\angle B+\angle C=180^\circ$,
     $\angle D+\angle F+\angle E=180^\circ$,
     $56+64+3x+15=180^\circ$,
     $3x+135=180^\circ$,
     $3x=54$, $x=15^\circ$

8) $\angle B=\angle D=110^\circ$,
     $\angle A=\angle E=40^\circ$,
     $\angle A+\angle B+\angle C=180^\circ$,
     $110^\circ+\angle C+40^\circ=180^\circ$,
     $\angle C=30^\circ$
     $\angle C=\angle F=30=2x-2$,
     $2x=32$, $x=16^\circ$

9) $\angle A=\angle E=90^\circ$,

$\angle D=\angle C=64^\circ$,
$\angle F=\angle B=26^\circ$,
$\angle B=2m+6=26^\circ$,
$2m=20$, $m=10^\circ$

10) $\angle A=\angle D=50^\circ$,
     $\angle C=\angle E=65^\circ$,
     $4m+5=65^\circ$, $4m=60^\circ$, $m=15^\circ$, $2m=30^\circ$

11) $\dfrac{7}{7+3}=\dfrac{8}{x} \Rightarrow \dfrac{7}{10}=\dfrac{8}{x}$, $x=\dfrac{80}{7}$

12) $\dfrac{4}{4+3}=\dfrac{6}{x} \Rightarrow \dfrac{4}{7}=\dfrac{6}{x}$, $x=\dfrac{42}{4}$, $x=\dfrac{21}{2}$

13) $\dfrac{8}{16}=\dfrac{12}{m} \Rightarrow \dfrac{1}{2}=\dfrac{12}{m} \Rightarrow m=24$

14) $\dfrac{8}{16}=\dfrac{4}{m} \Rightarrow \dfrac{1}{2}=\dfrac{4}{m} \Rightarrow m=8$

15) $\dfrac{6}{x}=\dfrac{4}{15} \Rightarrow 4x=90$, $x=22,5$

TEST– 7
(*Solutions*)

1) $\angle AB=\angle AC$, $\angle B=\angle C=x$,
    $\angle A+\angle B+\angle C=180°$,
    $80°+x+x=180°$, $2x=100°$, $x=50°$

2) $\angle AB=\angle AC$, $\angle B=\angle C=x$,
    $\angle A+\angle B+\angle C=180°$,
    $2x+x+x=180°$, $4x=100°$, $x=45°$
    $\angle B=\angle C=x=45°$

3) $AB=AC \Rightarrow \angle B=\angle C$,
    $\angle ACB+\angle ACD=180°$,
    $\angle ACB+134°=180° \Rightarrow \angle ACB=46°$,
    $\angle A+\angle B+\angle C=180°$,
    $\angle A+46°+46°=180°$, $\angle A=88°$

4) $AB=AC$, $\angle B=\angle C=2y$,
    $\angle A+\angle B+\angle C=180°$,
    $x+2y+2y=180° \Rightarrow x+4y=180°$, $x=180°-4y$

5) $AB=AC \Rightarrow 24=4x+4$, $4x=20$, $x=5$

6) $AB=AC \Rightarrow \angle B=\angle C=x$,
    $\angle A+\angle B+\angle C=180°$,
    $88+x+x=180°$, $x=46°$
    $\angle A-\angle C=88°-46°=42°$

7) $P(DEF)=2a+2a+2a=6a$,
    $P(ABC)=a+b+b=a+2b$,
    $P(DEF)-P(ABC)=6a-(a+2b)=5a-2b$

8) $DE=EF=FD \Rightarrow \angle E+\angle F+\angle D=60°$,
    $\angle B=\angle C=\dfrac{(180-86)}{2}=47$,
    $(LF):(LB)=\dfrac{60}{47}$

9) $AB=AC=BC$,
    $\angle A=\angle B=\angle C=60°=x$,
    $\angle C+y=180°$, $60°+y=180°$, $y=120°$
    $y-x=120°-60°=60°$

10) $AB=AC=BC=4$,
    $P(ABC)=4+4+x=8+x$,
    $P(DEF)=3(x+4)=3x+12$,
    $P(DEF)-P(ABC)=(3x+12)-(x+8)=2x+4$

11) $\angle AB=\angle AC$, $\angle B=\angle C$,
    $\angle A+\angle B+\angle C=180°$,
    $x+x+20°+x+20°=180°$, $3x=140°$, $x=\dfrac{140}{3}$

12) $P(ABD)=6+4+5=15$,
    $P(ADC)=4+6+5=15$,
    $P(ABC)=6+6+10=22$,
    $Sum=15+15+22=52$

13) $BC=a$, $CE=b$, $EK=c$
    All perimeter$=3a+3b+3c$
    $=3(a+b+c)=3\cdot12=36$

14) $\angle A=\angle C=45°$,
    $\angle D=\angle E=\angle F=60°$,
    $\angle F-\angle C=60°-45°=15°$

15) $\angle A=\angle C=\angle D=60°$,
    $2x+20°+120°=180$,
    $2x=40°$, $x=20°$

TEST– 8
(*Solutions*)

1) $\angle ABD=\angle DBC=3x+5$,
$3x+5+3x+5=90°$,
$6x+10=90°$, $x=\dfrac{80}{6}=\dfrac{40}{3}$

2) $2m+2n=180° \Rightarrow m+n=90°$

3) $2m+2n=90° \Rightarrow m+n=45°$

4) 15

5) $\dfrac{7}{3}=\dfrac{10}{DC} \Rightarrow DC=\dfrac{30}{7}$

6) $BD=DC$,
$6x-9=2x+11$,   ?
$4x=20$, $x=5$

7) $\angle ABD=\angle DBC$
$7x+10°=4x+40°$
$3x=30°$, $x=10°$

8) $\angle ABD=\angle DBC=\dfrac{124}{2}=62°$

9) $BD=DL=5$, $AE=EL=4$,
$DC:CE=\dfrac{5}{4}$

10) $BK=\dfrac{2}{3}BE=\dfrac{2}{3}\cdot 30=20$,
$AK=\dfrac{2}{3}AD=\dfrac{2}{3}\cdot 27=18$
$BK:AK=20:18=\dfrac{10}{9}$

11) $KF=\dfrac{1}{3}FB \Rightarrow \dfrac{FB}{3}=8$, $FB=24$
$KB=\dfrac{2}{3}FB=\dfrac{2}{3}\cdot 24=16\,cm$

12) $AF=DF=FL=18cm$,
$DF=\dfrac{1}{3}AF=\dfrac{18}{3}=6cm$

Solution is wrong.

13) $DE=\dfrac{1}{3}AD \Rightarrow \dfrac{AD}{3}=2\sqrt{3}$, $AD=6\sqrt{3}$

14) $\dfrac{10}{x}=\dfrac{8}{4} \Rightarrow x=5$

15) $\dfrac{5\sqrt{3}}{3\sqrt{3}}=\dfrac{6\sqrt{3}}{DC} \Rightarrow DC=\dfrac{18\sqrt{3}}{5}$

TEST– 9
(*Solutions*)

1) ∠A+∠B+∠C+∠D=360º
100+80+x+2x=360º,
3x=180º, x=60º

2) ∠A+∠B+∠C+∠D=360º
75+64+130+x=360º,
x=91º

3) ∠A+∠B+∠C+∠D=360º
∠A+130+115+73=360º,
∠A=42º

4) ∠A+∠B+∠C+∠D=360º
110+3x+3x+94=360º,
6x=156º, x=26º

5) ∠A+∠B+∠C+∠D=360º
90+88+94+2x=360º,
2x=88º, x=44º

6) ∠A+∠B+∠C+∠D=360º
4x+4x+3x+3x=360º,
14x=360º, x=$\dfrac{360}{14}=\dfrac{180}{7}$
∠A+∠D=4x+3x=7x=180º

7) ∠A+∠B+∠C+∠D=360º
54+64+∠C+120=360º,
∠C=122º

8) ∠A+∠B+∠C+∠D=360º
120+120+3x+3x=360º,
240+6x=360º, 6x=120º, x=20º

9) ∠A+∠B+∠C+∠D=360º
5x+80+64+7x=360º,
12x=216º, x=18º

10) ∠A+∠B+∠C+∠D+∠E+∠F=720º
∠A+∠E=240º

11) ∠A+∠B+∠C+∠D=360º
78+61+79+x=360º,
x=142º

12) ∠A+∠B+∠C+∠D=360º
74+74+2x+2x=360º,
4x=212º, x=53º

13) ∠A+∠B+∠C+∠D=360º
88+64+∠C+90=360º,
x=118º

14) ∠A+∠B+∠C+∠D=360º
x+113+63+33=360º,
x=151º

15) ∠A+∠B+∠C+∠D=360º
x+110+120+20=360º,
x=110º

TEST – 10
(*Solutions*)

1) $EF = \dfrac{BC}{2} = \dfrac{26}{2} = 13$

2) $DE = \dfrac{BC}{2} = 19$, $BC = 38$

3) $DE = \dfrac{BC}{2} = \dfrac{4x+6}{2} = 3x$, $2x+3=3x$, $x=3$

$BC+DE=18+9=27$

4) $DE = \dfrac{BC}{2} = \dfrac{3x+4}{2} = x+6$, $3x+4=2x+12$,

$x=8$

5) $KE = \dfrac{AC}{2} = 14$, $AC = 28$,

$KD = \dfrac{BC}{2} = 11$, $BC = 22$,

$AC+BC=50$

6) $DE = \dfrac{BC}{2} = 4x+6y$, $BC=8x+12y$

7) $DE = \dfrac{BC}{2} = 2^{12}$, $BC=2^{12}\cdot2^{1}$, $BC=2^{13}$

8) $FD = \dfrac{AC}{2} = 2^{x}$, $AC = 2^{x+1}$,

$FE = \dfrac{AB}{2} = 3^{x}$, $AB = 2\cdot3^{x}$,

$AC+AB=2^{x+1}+2\cdot3^{x}=2(2^{x}+3^{x})$

9) Midpoint $= \left(\dfrac{x_1 + x_2}{2} ; \dfrac{y_1 + y_2}{2} \right)$

$M_{AB} = \left(\dfrac{-8-6}{2} ; \dfrac{-10+14}{2} \right) = (-7, 2)$

10) Midpoint $= \left(\dfrac{x_1 + x_2}{2} ; \dfrac{y_1 + y_2}{2} \right) =$

$= \left(\dfrac{-6+4}{2} ; \dfrac{10+8}{2} \right) = (-1, 9)$

11)

A(4, 2)　　　K(–2, 3)　　　B(x, y)

$\dfrac{x+4}{2} = -2$, $\quad$ x=–8,

$\dfrac{2+y}{2} = 3$, $\quad$ y=4,

$B(x, y) \Rightarrow B(-8, 4)$

12) Midpoint$(x, y) = \left(\dfrac{-4-6}{2} ; \dfrac{8+12}{2} \right)$

$=(-5; 10)$

13) Midpoint$(x, y) = \left(\dfrac{-2+6}{2} ; \dfrac{6+7}{2} \right) = \left(2; \dfrac{13}{2} \right)$

14) Midpoint$(x, y) = \left(\dfrac{-3+5}{2} ; \dfrac{-10-2}{2} \right)$

$=(1; -6)$

15) Midpoint $D = \left(\dfrac{20-12}{2} ; \dfrac{10-6}{2} \right) = (4, 2)$

Midpoint $E = \left(\dfrac{4+20}{2} ; \dfrac{2-6}{2} \right) = (12, -2)$

TEST– 11
(*Solutions*)

1) $\angle A=68^o$, $\angle A+\angle B=180^o$, $\angle B=112^o$,
    $\angle B-\angle C=112-68=44^o$, $\angle A=\angle C$

2) $\angle A+\angle B=180^o$, $2x+124^0=180^o$, $2x=56^0$,
    $x=28^0$

3) 6

4) $\angle A=\angle C=3x$, , $\angle B=\angle D=111$,
    $\angle A+\angle B=180^o$, $3x+111=180$, $3x=69$, $x=23$
    Angle A= Angle C=3x=3x 23=69

5) $\angle A=\angle C=66^o$, $3m=66$, $m=22$,
    $\angle A+\angle B=180^o$, $66+3n=180$, $3n=114$, $n=38$
    $n+m=38+22=60$

6) $\angle CBA+\angle CBE=180^o$,
    $\angle CBA+64^o=180^o$, $\angle CBA=116^o$,
    $\angle D=\angle CBA=116^o$, $\angle A=\angle CBE=64^o$,
    $\angle D-\angle A=116-64=52^o$

7) $AB=DC$, $24=3x$, $x=8$,
    $AD=BC$, $2y=2\sqrt{6}$, $y=\sqrt{6}$
    $x+y=8+\sqrt{6}$

8) $mx=6x$, $m=6$,
    $ny=2y$, $n=2$
    $4m+3n=4\cdot6+3\cdot2=30$

9) $\angle A+\angle B=180^o$, $125+x=180^o$, $x=55^o$

10) $\angle A+\angle B=180^o$, $8n+4m=180^o$,
    $\dfrac{8m+4n}{4}=\dfrac{180}{4}$, $2n+m=45^o$

11) $P(ABCD)=P(a+b)=2(6+8)=28$

12) $P(ABCD)=2(2^8+2^6) \Rightarrow$
    $2^7+2^6=2^A\cdot B$,
    $2^6(2^1+1)=2^A\cdot B$
    $3\cdot2^7=2^A\cdot B$,
    $A=7$, $B=3$, $A+B=10$

13) $P_1(ABCD)=2(10+6)=32$
    $P_2(ABFE)=2(10+3)=26$
    $P_3(FEDC)=(10+3)\cdot2=26$
    $P_1+P_2+P_3=32+26+26=84$

14) $EC=AE=\sqrt{24}$,
    $DE=EB=\sqrt{12}$,
    $AC+BD=2\sqrt{24}+2\sqrt{12}=$
    $=4\sqrt{6}+4\sqrt{3}=4(\sqrt{6}+\sqrt{3})$

15) $AE=EC=3^x$, $AC=2\cdot3^x$,
    $BE=ED=3^x \Rightarrow BD=2\cdot3^x$
    $|AC|\cdot|BD|=(2\cdot3^x)\cdot(2\cdot3^x)$
    $4\cdot3^{2x}=A\cdot3^{2x}$,
    $A=4$, $B=2$, $A+B=6$

TEST– 12
(*Solutions*)

1) AB=BC, 3y=2y+6, y=6
   DC=3y=6·3=18

2) 5

3) $\angle$BAC=3x=45º, x=15
   $\angle$ABC=90º=3y, y=30
   y–x=30–15=15

4) $\angle$A=$\angle$C, 64=2x, x=32

5) $AE=EC=\dfrac{AC}{2}=\dfrac{\sqrt{54}}{2}=\dfrac{3\sqrt{6}}{2}$

   $BE=ED=\dfrac{BD}{2}=\dfrac{\sqrt{24}}{2}=\dfrac{2\sqrt{6}}{2}=\sqrt{6}$

   $2AE=\dfrac{3\sqrt{6}}{2}-\sqrt{6}=3\sqrt{6}-\sqrt{6}=2\sqrt{6}$

6) AB=DC, 3x+6=30, 3x=24, x=8
   AD=BC, 25=5y+5, 5y=20, y=4
   2x+y=2·8+4=20

7) $\dfrac{P(ABCD)}{P(KLMN)}=\dfrac{2(8+6)}{4\sqrt{28}}=\dfrac{28}{8\sqrt{7}}=\dfrac{7}{2\sqrt{7}}$
   $=\sqrt{7}/2$

8) $\dfrac{P(KLMN)}{P(ABCD)}=\dfrac{4\cdot 9^{x}}{4\cdot 3^{x}}=3^{x}$

9) P(ABCD)+P(KLMN)=32,

   2(a+b)+4·a=32,
   2a+2b+4a=32,
   6a+2b=32,
   3a+b=16

10) $\dfrac{P(KLMN)}{P(ABCD)}=\dfrac{4\cdot 4^{x}}{4\cdot 4}=\dfrac{4^{x}}{4}=4^{x-1}$

   $\dfrac{P(ABCD)}{P(KLMN)}=\dfrac{4\cdot 4^{x}}{4\cdot 4}=\dfrac{4^{x}}{4}=4^{x-1}$

11) AE=EC=4cm,
    BD=AC=8cm,
    AC=8cm

12) $AE=EC=\dfrac{AC}{2}=\dfrac{18}{2}=9$

    $BE=ED=\dfrac{BD}{2}=\dfrac{24}{2}=12$

    BE+EC=12+9=21

13) $AC=2\sqrt{6}$,
    $|AB|^{2}+|BC|^{2}=\left(2\sqrt{6}\right)^{2}$
    $a^{2}+a^{2}=24$, $2a^{2}=24$, $a^{2}=12$, $a=2\sqrt{3}$,
    $P(ABCD)=4a=4\cdot 2\sqrt{3}=8\sqrt{3}cm$

14) $AC=BD=\sqrt{2^{2}+1^{2}}=\sqrt{5}$,
    $\dfrac{P(ABCD)}{(AC+BD)}=\dfrac{2\cdot(2+1)}{\sqrt{5}+\sqrt{5}}=\dfrac{6}{2\sqrt{5}}=\dfrac{3}{\sqrt{5}}$

15) $|AB|^{2}+|BC|^{2}=|AC|^{2}$,
    $16^{2}+12^{2}=(AC)^{2}\Rightarrow AC=20$
    $AE=EC=\dfrac{AC}{2}=\dfrac{20}{2}=10$
    $|AE|:|BC|=\dfrac{10}{12}=\dfrac{5}{6}$

TEST– 13
(*Solutions*)

1) If AD=BC,
   $\angle A = \angle B = 48^\circ$

2) EF$= \dfrac{AB+DC}{2} = \dfrac{14+8}{2} = 11$

3) $\angle D = \angle C = 46^\circ$,
   $\angle B + \angle C = 180^\circ$,
   $\angle B = 134^\circ$

4) EF$= \dfrac{AB+DC}{2} = \dfrac{6x+10+2x+4}{2}$
   EF$= \dfrac{8x+14}{2} = 4x+7$

5) EF$= \dfrac{BC+AD}{2} = 14$, $\dfrac{6+AD}{2} = 14$,
   AD+6=28, AD=22

6) EF$= \dfrac{AB+DC}{2} = 12$, $\dfrac{6x+2+2x+6}{2} = 12$,
   8x+8=24, 8x=16, x=2

7) $\angle A + \angle B + \angle C + \angle D = 360^\circ$
   $\angle A = \angle C = x$,
   $\angle A + 130 + \angle C + 40 = 360^\circ$,
   2x+170=360°, 2x=190°, x=95°

8) $\angle A + \angle B + \angle C + \angle D = 360^\circ$, $\angle B = \angle D$
   80+112+$\angle C$+112=360°, $\angle C = 56^\circ$

9)

   $\dfrac{4}{10} = \dfrac{x-8}{4}$,
   10x–80=16,
   10x=96, x=9,6

10) 64+n+n=180°,
    2n=116, n=58°,
    n+2x=180°, 58+2x=180, 2x=122, x=61

11) $\dfrac{DC}{AB} = \dfrac{1}{7} = \dfrac{1x}{7x}$, EF$= \dfrac{x+7x}{2} = 4x$
    $\dfrac{EF}{AB+DC} = \dfrac{4x}{7x+x} = \dfrac{4x}{8x} = \dfrac{1}{2}$

12) 3α+2α=180, 5α=180, α=36°

13) EF$= \dfrac{AB+DC}{2} = \dfrac{mx+nx}{2}$

14) EF$= \dfrac{AB+DC}{2} = \dfrac{2^{2x+2}+2^{x+1}}{2} = 2^{2x+1}+2^x$

15) EF$= \dfrac{AB+DC}{2} = 22$, AB+DC=44,
    P(ABCD)=AB+DC+BC+AD
    =44+16+10=70

TEST– 14
(*Solutions*)

1) $A(ABC) = \dfrac{AB \cdot CD}{2} = \dfrac{12 \cdot 4}{2} = 24$

2) $A(ABC) = \dfrac{AB \cdot BC}{2} = \dfrac{14 \cdot 6}{2} = 42$

3) $A(ABC) = \dfrac{AB \cdot BC}{2} = \dfrac{(x+4) \cdot 6}{2} = 24$,

$6(x+4)=48$, $x+4=8$, $x=4$

4) $A(ABC) = \dfrac{DC \cdot AB}{2} = 36$, $DC \cdot 12 = 72$,

$DC = 6$

5) $A(ABC) = \dfrac{AB \cdot BC}{2} = \dfrac{(x+6) \cdot (x+4)}{2} = 24$,

$x^2 + 4x + 6x + 24 = 48$,

$x^2 + 10 - 24 = 0$, $(x+12) \cdot (x-2) = 0$,

$-12 \quad\quad x = -12$,

$-2 \quad\quad x = 2$

$AB + BC = x + 6 + x + 4 = 2x + 10 = 14$

6) $A(ABC) = \dfrac{a^2\sqrt{3}}{4} = \dfrac{10^2\sqrt{3}}{4} = 25\sqrt{3}$

7) $A(ABC) = \dfrac{AB \cdot BC}{2} = 12$,

$\angle A = \angle C = 45^\circ$, $AB = BC = x$,

$\dfrac{x \cdot x}{2} = 12$, $x^2 = 24$, $x = 2\sqrt{6}$

8) $A(ABC) = \dfrac{6 \cdot 8 \cdot \sin\alpha}{2} =$

$= 24 \cdot \sin\alpha = 24 \cdot \sin 30^\circ = 12\,\text{cm}^2$

9)

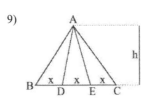

$BD = DE = EC = x$,

$A(ABD) = \dfrac{x \cdot h}{2} = 6$,

$x \cdot h = 12$,

$A(ABC) = \dfrac{3x \cdot h}{2} =$

$= \dfrac{3 \cdot 12}{2} = 18\,\text{cm}^2$

10) $\dfrac{BD}{DC} = \dfrac{3}{5} = \dfrac{3x}{5x}$

$\dfrac{3x}{A(ABD)} = \dfrac{5x}{A(ADC)}$, $\dfrac{3}{15} = \dfrac{5}{A(ADC)}$

$A(ADC) = 25\,\text{cm}^2$, $A(ABC) = 25 + 15 = 40\,\text{cm}^2$

11) $A(ADC) = \dfrac{AB \cdot DC}{2} = 24$, $\dfrac{8 \cdot DC}{2} = 24$

$DC = 6$

12) $A(ABC) = \dfrac{AC \cdot BD}{2} = \dfrac{AE \cdot 10}{2}$,

$16 \cdot 6 = AE \cdot 10$, $AE = 9{,}6$

13) $A(ABC) = 4 \cdot 7 = 28 cm^2$

14) $\dfrac{CD}{DB} = \dfrac{3}{7} = \dfrac{3x}{7x}$,

$A(ABC) = 10x$,

$60 = 10x$, $x = 10 cm^2$

$A(ACD) = 10x = 30 cm^2$

15) $AD = h$,

$\dfrac{A(ABD)}{A(ADC)} = \dfrac{\dfrac{BD \cdot h}{2}}{\dfrac{DC \cdot h}{2}} = \dfrac{\dfrac{\sqrt{6}h}{2}}{\dfrac{\sqrt{12}h}{2}}$

$= \dfrac{\sqrt{6}}{\sqrt{12}} = \dfrac{1}{\sqrt{2}}$

TEST – 15
(*Solutions*)

1) $A(ABCD) = \dfrac{AC^2}{2} = \dfrac{(20)^2}{2} = \dfrac{400}{2} = 200$

2) $P(ABCD) = 4a$, $44 = 4a$, $a = 11cm$,
$S(ABCD) = a^2 = (11)^2 = 121cm^2$

3) $4a = 4\pi$, $a = \pi cm$,
$S(ABCD) = a^2 = (\pi)^2 = \pi^2 cm^2$

4) $A(ABCD) = a^2 = (7^x)^2 = 7^{2x} cm$

5) $\dfrac{A(ABCD)}{P(ABCD)} = \dfrac{a^2}{4a} = \dfrac{a}{4} = \dfrac{3\pi}{4}$

6) $AE = EC = 4cm$, $AC = BD = 8cm$,
$A(ABCD) = \dfrac{a^2}{2} = \dfrac{(8)^2}{2} = \dfrac{64}{2} = 32cm^2$

7) $A(ABCD) = 4 \cdot A(BEC) = 4 \cdot 22 = 88cm^2$
$A(DAB) = \dfrac{A(ABCD)}{2} = \dfrac{88}{2} = 44cm^2$

8) $\dfrac{P(ABCD)}{A(ABCD)} = \dfrac{4a}{a^2} = \dfrac{4}{a} = \dfrac{4}{2^x}$

9) $A(ABE) = \dfrac{A(ABCD)}{2} = 50$,
$A(ABCD) = 100cm^2$,
$a^2 = 100$, $a = 10cm$,
$P(ABCD) = 4a = 4 \cdot 10 = 40cm$

10) $A(BEC) = \dfrac{A(ABCD)}{4} = 36$,
$A(ABCD) = 4 \cdot 36 \Rightarrow A(ABCD) = 144$,
$a^2 = 144$, $a = 12cm$, $P = 4a = 4 \cdot 12 = 48cm$

11) All area $= 16 + 4 + 4 + 4 + 4 = 32cm^2$

12) $A(ABCD) = 289 = a^2$, $a = 17cm$,
$A(LKEF) = 400$, $b^2 = 400$, $b = 20cm$
$\dfrac{P(ABCD)}{P(LKFE)} = \dfrac{4a}{4b} = \dfrac{a}{b} = \dfrac{17}{20}$

13) Drawn area $= (AB)^2 - (EK)^2 =$
$= 12^2 - 6^2 = 144 - 36 = 108cm^2$

14) $P(ABCD) = 4a = 8\sqrt{3}$, $\Rightarrow a = 2\sqrt{3}$,
$P(EFKL) = 4b = 4\sqrt{2}$, $\Rightarrow b = \sqrt{2}$,
$\dfrac{A(ABCD)}{A(EFKL)} = \dfrac{a^2}{b^2} = \dfrac{(2\sqrt{3})^2}{(\sqrt{2})^2} = \dfrac{12}{2} = 6$

15) $\dfrac{A(ABCD)}{A(LKFE)} = \dfrac{\dfrac{14^2}{2}}{\dfrac{8^2}{2}} = \dfrac{196}{64} = \dfrac{49}{16}$

TEST– 16
(*Solutions*)

1) P(ABCD)=2(a+b)=2(x+4+x+2)
   =2(2x+6)=4x+12

2) P(ABCD)=2(a+b), 30=2(3x+2x), 15=5x,
   x=3
   A(ABCD)=AB·BC=3x·2x=6x²=6·3²=54

3) $\dfrac{A(ABCD)}{P(ABCD)} = \dfrac{AB \cdot BC}{2(AB + BC)}$

   $= \dfrac{10 \cdot 6}{2(10 + 6)} = \dfrac{60}{32} = \dfrac{15}{8}$

4) A(ABCD)=AB·BC, 18=2x·x, 2x²=18,
   x²=9, x=3
   P(ABCD)=2(2x+x)=6x=6·3=18

5) $|AB|^2+|BC|^2=|AC|^2$, $|AB|^2+5^2=13^2$
   $\Rightarrow$ AB=12,
   P(ABCD)=2(AB+BC)=2(12+5)=34

6) $|AB|^2+|BC|^2=|AC|^2$, $16^2+12^2=|AC|^2$
   $\Rightarrow$ AC=20,
   $\dfrac{P(ABCD)}{P(BAC)} = \dfrac{2(16+12)}{16+12+20} = \dfrac{2 \cdot 28}{48} = \dfrac{7}{6}$

7) $\dfrac{A(ABCD)}{A(ABC)} = \dfrac{8 \cdot 10}{\dfrac{8 \cdot 10}{2}} = \dfrac{80}{40} = 2$

8) Diagonal $= x = \sqrt{5^2 + 3^2} = \sqrt{34}$

9)

   P=2(a+b), 200=2(x+3x),
   100=4x, x=25,
   A(ABCD)=3x·x=3x²=
   =3·25²=3·625=1875

10) $|DE|^2$=AE·EC, $|DE|^2$=3·8 $\Rightarrow$
    $\Rightarrow$ DE= $2\sqrt{6}$

11) $\dfrac{A(ABD)}{A(BCD)} = \dfrac{\dfrac{4 \cdot 5}{2}}{\dfrac{3 \cdot 5}{2}} = \dfrac{4 \cdot 5}{3 \cdot 5} = \dfrac{4}{3}$

12) A(ABD)= $\dfrac{AB \cdot DC}{2}$ =10, $\dfrac{5 \cdot DC}{2}$ =10,
    DC=4cm
    A(ACDE)=AC·DC=13·4=52cm²

13) Striped area = mn–xy

14) $\dfrac{P(ABCD)}{P(EFKL)} = \dfrac{2(2m + 2n)}{2(m + n)} = 2$

15) ∠ALE=∠CAE=23°,
    ∠CEB=23+23=46°

TEST – 17
(*Solutions*)

1) ∠ABC=∠ADB+∠BDC=74°+34°=108°

2) DC=AB=12=x,
AD=BC=7=m,
AE=EC=6=a,
(x+m+a)=(12+7+6)=25

3) AB=DC, 3y=18, y=6,
AD=BC, 8=3x–4, 12=3x, x=4
(x+y)=(6+4)=10

4) ∠A=∠D=180°,
3x+6x=180°,
9x=180°,
x=20°

5) AB=DC, 4x–4=24, 4x=28, x=7
$(2x^2+2)=(2\cdot7^2+2)=(2\cdot49+2)=100$

6) A(ABCD)=Base · x height = 13·6=78cm²

7) A(ABCD)=AB·DE=10·4=40cm²

8) A(ABCD)=BC·DE=8·12=96cm²

9) A(ABCD)=AB·DE=BC·DF, 16·10=BC·14,
80=7BC, BC=$\dfrac{80}{7}$, AD = BC = $\dfrac{80}{7}$

10) ∠A=∠y=66°, x+y=180, x+66=180,
x=114°,
x–y=114–66, x–y=48

11) P=2(a+b), $\dfrac{a}{b} = \dfrac{11}{13} = \dfrac{11k}{13k}$,
P=2(a+b)=2(11k+13k)=2·24k=48k,
k=1, for P(ABCD)=48k=48cm

12) A(ADE)= $\dfrac{A(ABCD)}{4} = 9$,
A(ABCD)=4·9=36cm²

13) A(ABCD)=a·h=14· $2\sqrt{3} = 28\sqrt{3}$ cm²

14) AK=KC=12, AC=12+12=24,
BK=KD=7, BD=7+7=14,
$\dfrac{AC}{BD} = \dfrac{24}{14} = \dfrac{12}{7}$

15) $\dfrac{AB}{BC} = \dfrac{a}{b} = \dfrac{1}{3} = \dfrac{x}{3x}$,
P(ABCD)=2(a+b)=60°,
2(x+3x)=60, 4x=30, x=7,5
BC=AD=x=7,5cm

TEST– 18
(*Solutions*)

1) P(ABCD)=4a=4·13=52

2) P(ABCD)=4a=60 $\Rightarrow$ a=15cm

3) P(ABCD)=4a=4π–4,

$a=\dfrac{4\pi-4}{4}=\pi-1$

4) A(ABCD)=$\dfrac{f\cdot e}{2}=\dfrac{10\cdot 14}{2}=70$,

e and f are diagonals.

5) P=(ABCD)=4a=4^{m+1},
4a=4^m·4, a=4^m

6) $e^2+f^2=4a^2$, $12^2+16^2=4a^2$,
144+256=$4a^2$, 400=$4a^2$, a^2=100, a=10
P(ABCD)=4a=4·10=40

7) A(ABCD)=a^2·sinα=

=$\left(10\sqrt{2}\right)^2\cdot\sin 45^\circ=100\cdot 2\cdot\dfrac{\sqrt{2}}{2}=100\sqrt{2}$

8) e and f are diagonal of rhombus.
$e^2+f^2=4a^2$, $10^2+24^2=4a^2$,
100+576=$4a^2$, 676=$4a^2$,
a^2=169, a=13

9) e=36, f=48, $e^2+f^2=4a^2$,
$36^2+48^2=4a^2$,
a=30cm

10) AC=e=12, BD=f=6, BC=a,
$e^2+f^2=4a^2$, $12^2+6^2=4a^2$, 180=$4a^2$, 45=a^2,
a= $3\sqrt{5}$, BC=a= $3\sqrt{5}$

11) A(ABCD)=DC·FE=8·9=72cm^2

12) A(ABCD)=a·h=16·9=144cm^2

13) A(ABCD)=a·h=5· $4\sqrt{3}=20\sqrt{3}$ cm^2

14) e=12, f=8, $e^2+f^2=4a^2$, $12^2+8^2=4a^2$,
144+64=$4a^2$, a^2=52, a= $2\sqrt{13}$
P(ABCD)=4a=4· $2\sqrt{13}=8\sqrt{13}$

15) A(ABCD)=a·h,
$20\sqrt{3}=10$·h,
h= $2\sqrt{3}$ cm^2

TEST– 19
(*Solutions*)

1) A$'$=(9,0)

2) B$'$=(6, 7)

3) A$'$=(14, 8)

4) B$'$=(8, 12)

5) K$'$=(0, 4)

6) N$'$=(0, –4)

7) A=(–3, 4)

8) 12=3y, y=4

9) 6=2x, x=3, x+y=3+4=7

10) 18=3x, x=6

11) 16=4y, y=4
   2x+2y=2(x+y)=2(6+4)=20

12) A$'$=(8, 0)

13) M$'$=(4, 10)

14) M=(–3, –7)

15) N$'$=(–4, –3)

TEST– 20
(*Solutions*)

1) (x+7; y–3)

2) (x+12; y+6)

3) (x–7; y–10)

4) $\overrightarrow{AB}$; (3; 3)

5) $\overrightarrow{CD}$; (–3;–3)

6) (x, y) → (x–4; y–5)

7) (8; 2)

8) (10; 7)

9) (10; 12)

10) (x, y) → (–4; –5)

11) A(-4, -2).
5 unit right 10 unit down (-4+5; -2-10)
A(1; -12)

12) 6 unit left, 8 unit down ⇒ (-6; -8)

13) 6 unit right, 14 unit down ⇒ <6; -14>

14) (x, y) → (x+4; y-2)
(8, 10) → (8+4; 10-2) ⇒ (12; 8)

15) (x, y) → (x-6; y+4)
(13, -6) → (12-6; -6+4) ⇒ (7; -2)

TEST– 21
(Solutions)

1) DC=x, AD=24–x,
$\dfrac{4}{16}=\dfrac{x}{24-x}$, $\dfrac{1}{4}=\dfrac{x}{24-x}$, 5x=24, x=4,8

2) $\dfrac{20}{12}=\dfrac{24}{x}$, $\Rightarrow x=14,4$

3) AB∥DC, if ∠B=∠C,
∠A+∠B+∠E=180°, 46^0+∠B+34=180°,
∠B=80°

4) $\dfrac{AD}{BD}=\dfrac{AE}{EC}\Rightarrow\dfrac{6}{9}=\dfrac{AE}{12}$,
$\dfrac{6}{3}=\dfrac{AE}{4}\Rightarrow AE=8$

5) $\dfrac{AD}{AB}=\dfrac{AE}{AC}\Rightarrow\dfrac{10}{10+16}=\dfrac{x}{24}$
$\dfrac{10}{26}=\dfrac{x}{24}\Rightarrow\dfrac{5}{13}=\dfrac{x}{12}\Rightarrow x=\dfrac{60}{13}$
EC= $24-\dfrac{60}{13}=\dfrac{312-60}{13}=\dfrac{252}{13}$

6) $\dfrac{24}{24+16}=\dfrac{ED}{BC}\Rightarrow\dfrac{24}{40}=\dfrac{ED}{28}$
$\dfrac{24}{10}=\dfrac{ED}{7}\Rightarrow ED=\dfrac{42}{10}$, ED=4,2

7) $\dfrac{14}{10}=\dfrac{x}{28-x}$, $\dfrac{7}{5}=\dfrac{x}{28-x}$
5x=196–7x, 12x=196, x=$\dfrac{196}{12}$, x=$\dfrac{49}{3}$

8) $\dfrac{8}{12}=\dfrac{9}{x}$, $\dfrac{2}{3}=\dfrac{9}{x}$, x=$\dfrac{27}{2}$

9) $\dfrac{A(ABC)}{A(DEF)}=\left(\dfrac{5}{3}\right)^2=\dfrac{25}{9}$

10) $\dfrac{A(ABC)}{A(DEF)}=k^2$, $\dfrac{4}{A(DEF)}=\left(\dfrac{2}{5}\right)^2$,
$\dfrac{4}{A(DEF)}=\dfrac{4}{25}\Rightarrow A(DEF)=25cm^2$

11) $\dfrac{6}{10}=\dfrac{x}{12-x}$, $\Rightarrow\dfrac{3}{5}=\dfrac{x}{12-x}$, x=$\dfrac{9}{2}$

12) $\dfrac{AD}{AC}=\dfrac{DE}{BC}\Rightarrow\dfrac{12}{28}=\dfrac{DE}{18}\Rightarrow x=\dfrac{54}{7}$=7.7

13) $A(ADE)=\dfrac{A(ABC)}{4}=5\Rightarrow$
$A(ABC)=4\cdot5=20cm^2$

14) $FE=\dfrac{AB}{2}=4$, $AB=8$,
$DE=\dfrac{BC}{2}=6$, $BC=12$
AB+BC=8+12=20

15) $\dfrac{x}{y}=\dfrac{3}{6}$, $\dfrac{x}{y}=\dfrac{1}{2}$, y=2x

TEST– 22
(*Solutions*)

1) $x^2 = 4^2 + 7^2 = \sqrt{65}$

2) $12^2 + 9^2 = (3x)^2$, $144 + 81 = (9x^2)$,
$225 = 9x^2$, $3x = 15$, $x = 5$
$2x + 2 = 2 \cdot 5 + 2 = 12$

3) $AC^2 = \left(\dfrac{1}{3}\right)^2 + \left(\dfrac{3}{4}\right)^2$, $AC^2 = \dfrac{1}{9} + \dfrac{9}{16}$,
$AC^2 = \dfrac{16 + 81}{144}$, $AC = \dfrac{\sqrt{97}}{12}$

4) $|AD|^2 = |AB|^2 + |BD|^2$,
$\left(\sqrt{208}\right)^2 = 12^2 + |BD|^2$
$208 = 144 + |BD|^2$, $BD = 8$cm, $DC = 8 - 5 = 3$

5) $|AC|^2 = |5^2| + 3^2$, $AC^2 = 25 + 9$, $AC = \sqrt{34}$
$|AB|^2 + |BC|^2 = |AC|^2$, $AB^2 + 2^2 = (\sqrt{34})^2$,
$AB = \sqrt{30}$

6) $|AB|^2 + |BC|^2 = |AC|^2$, $|3x|^2 + |BC|^2 = |4x|^2$,
$|BC|^2 = 16x^2 - 9x^2$, $BC = x\sqrt{7}$

7) $|AC|^2 = (2x)^2 + (6x)^2$, $AC^2 = 4x^2 + 36x^2$,
$AC = 2x\sqrt{10}$
$P(ABCD) = 6x + 2x + 2x\sqrt{10} = 8x + 2x\sqrt{10}$

8) $|AD|^2 = |AB|^2 - |BD|^2 = 6^2 - 4^2$, $AD = 2\sqrt{5}$
$|AD|^2 + |DC|^2 = x^2$, $\left(2\sqrt{5}\right)^2 + 2^2 = x^2$,
$x = 2\sqrt{6}$

9) $|BD|^2 = 6^2 - 4^2 \Rightarrow BD = 2\sqrt{5}$,
$|DC|^2 = 7^2 - 4^2 \Rightarrow DC = \sqrt{33}$,
$BD:DC = 2\sqrt{5} : \sqrt{33}$

10) $|AD|^2 = 5 \cdot 8 \Rightarrow AD = 2\sqrt{10}$,
$A(ABC) = \dfrac{13 \cdot 2\sqrt{10}}{2} = 13\sqrt{10}$,
$\dfrac{AD}{A(ABC)} = \dfrac{2\sqrt{10}}{13\sqrt{10}} = \dfrac{2}{13}$

11) $AB^2 = 3x(3x + 4x) = 3x \cdot 7x$, $AB = x\sqrt{21}$,
$AC^2 = 4x(4x + 3x) \Rightarrow AC^2 = 4x \cdot 7x$,
$AC = 2x\sqrt{7}$
$\dfrac{AB}{AC} = \dfrac{x\sqrt{21}}{2x\sqrt{7}} = \dfrac{\sqrt{3}}{2}$

12) $AC = \sqrt{(4a)^2 + a^2} = a\sqrt{17}$,
$P(ABC) = a + 4a + a\sqrt{17} = 5a + a\sqrt{17}$

13) $BC = 3x\sqrt{3}$,
$\dfrac{BC}{P(ABC)} = \dfrac{3x\sqrt{3}}{9x + 3x\sqrt{3}} = \dfrac{\sqrt{3}}{3 + \sqrt{3}}$

14) $AC = \sqrt{7^2 + 3^2} = \sqrt{58}$,
$\dfrac{AC}{A(ABC)} = \dfrac{\sqrt{58}}{\frac{7 \cdot 3}{2}} = \dfrac{2\sqrt{58}}{21}$

15) $|AD|^2 = (4a) \cdot (6a)$, $AD = \sqrt{24a^2} = 2a\sqrt{6}$

TEST– 23
(*Solutions*)

1) $|AB|^2+|BC|^2=|AC|^2$, $5^2+5^2=|AC|^2$,
 $AC=5\sqrt{2}$

2) $|AB|^2+|BC|^2=|AC|^2$, $AB=BC=x$,
 $x^2+x^2=\left(7\sqrt{2}\right)^2$,
 $2x^2=49\cdot2$, $x=7$, $AB+BC=7+7=14$

3) $AB=BC=x$, $x^2+x^2=14^2$, $\Rightarrow$
 $2x^2=196$, $x^2=98$, $x=7\sqrt{2}$
 $A(ABC)=\dfrac{x\cdot x}{2}=\dfrac{7\sqrt{2}\cdot7\sqrt{2}}{2}=49$

4) $|AC|^2=(3x)^2+(3x)^2 \Rightarrow AC=3x\sqrt{2}$
 $\dfrac{P(ABC)}{AC}=\dfrac{3x+3x+3x\sqrt{2}}{3x\sqrt{2}}=$
 $=\dfrac{1+1+\sqrt{2}}{\sqrt{2}}=\dfrac{2+\sqrt{2}}{2}$

5) $AB=BC=x$,
 if $\dfrac{x\cdot x}{2}=10$, $x^2=20$, $x=2\sqrt{5}$
 $AC=\sqrt{x^2+x^2}=\sqrt{20+20}=2\sqrt{10}$,
 $P(ABC)=2\sqrt{5}+2\sqrt{5}+2\sqrt{10}$
 $=4\sqrt{5}+2\sqrt{10}$

6) $AB=AC=x$, $BC=\sqrt{x^2+x^2}$,
 $20^2=x^2+x^2$, $\Rightarrow 400=2x^2$, $200=x^2$, $x=10\sqrt{2}$
 $\dfrac{AB+AC}{BC}=\dfrac{x+x}{20}=\dfrac{2x}{20}$
 $=\dfrac{x}{10}=\dfrac{10\sqrt{2}}{10}=\sqrt{2}$

7) $AC=18cm$, $AB=9$, $BC=9\sqrt{3}$,
 $\dfrac{BC}{AB}=\dfrac{9\sqrt{3}}{9}=\sqrt{3}$

8) $AB=\dfrac{BC}{2}=8$, $AB=16$,
 $BC=\dfrac{AB}{2}\sqrt{3}=\dfrac{16}{2}\sqrt{3}=8\sqrt{3}$,
 $A(ABC)=\dfrac{AB\cdot BC}{2}=\dfrac{8\cdot8\sqrt{3}}{2}=32\sqrt{3}$

9) $AB=\dfrac{6x}{2}=3x$, $BC=\dfrac{6x}{2}\sqrt{3}=3x\sqrt{3}$,
 $A(ABC)=\dfrac{3x\cdot3x\sqrt{3}}{2}=\dfrac{9x^2\sqrt{3}}{2}$

10) $DC=AC$, if $\angle D=\angle A=30º$,
 $\angle C=(30+30)º=60º$,
 $\angle CAB=30º$, $AC=4cm$,
 $BC=\dfrac{AC}{2}=\dfrac{4}{2}=2$

11) $\angle D=(15+30)=45°$,
    $\angle BAD=\angle BDA=45°$,
    $|AD|^2=AB^2+BD^2=6^2+6^2$, $AD=6\sqrt{2}$

12) $DC=\dfrac{AD}{2}=\dfrac{6}{2}=3cm$,

    $AC=\dfrac{AD}{2}\sqrt{3}=3\sqrt{3}$,

    $\angle CBA=\angle BAC=45°$ if $BC=AC=3\sqrt{3}$
    $AB=\sqrt{27+27}=3\sqrt{6}$

13) $BC^2=3^2+12^2=225$, $BC=15$,
    $AD=\dfrac{9\cdot12}{15}=\dfrac{3\cdot12}{5}=\dfrac{36}{5}$

14) $BC=BD=x$, $x^2+x^2=4^2$, $x=2\sqrt{2}$,
    $\dfrac{AB}{BC}=\dfrac{2+2\sqrt{2}}{2\sqrt{2}}=\dfrac{1+\sqrt{2}}{\sqrt{2}}$

15) $AC=\sqrt{(3x)^2+(3y)^2}$,
    $AC=\sqrt{9x^2+9y^2}=\sqrt{9(x^2+y^2)}$
    $AC=3\sqrt{x^2+y^2}$

TEST– 24
(*Solutions*)

1) $\vec{A} = 2i+4j \Rightarrow 3\vec{A} = (6i+12j)$
$\vec{B} = (3i+3j) \Rightarrow 2\vec{B} = (6i+6j)$
$3\vec{A} + 2\vec{B} = 12i+18j$

2) $\vec{A} - \vec{B} = \sqrt{(9-6)^2 + (5-1)^2} =$
$\sqrt{9+16}$
$\vec{A} - \vec{B} = 5$

3) $\text{Area} = \dfrac{(60+40)\cdot(8-4)}{2} = \dfrac{100\cdot 4}{2} = 200$

4) $\vec{A} = \sqrt{4^2 + (-2)^2 + 3^2} = \sqrt{16+4+9} = \sqrt{29}$
$\vec{A} = \sqrt{29}$

5) $\vec{A} = (4i;\ 6j),\ \vec{B} = (2i;\ -2j),$
$\overrightarrow{AB} = (4i-2i;\ 6j+2j),\ \overrightarrow{AB} = (2i;\ 8j)$

6) $\vec{A} = \sqrt{a^2 + b^2} = \sqrt{6^2 + (-8)^2} = \sqrt{100}$,
$\vec{A} = 10$

7) $\vec{A} = (-6;\ 4),\ \vec{B} = (7;\ 5),$
$\vec{A} + \vec{B} = (-6+7;\ 4+5) = (1;\ 9)$

8) $|\vec{A}| = \sqrt{a^2 + b^2} = \sqrt{3^2 + 5^2} = \sqrt{34}$

9) $\vec{A} = (9;\ 4),\ 5\vec{A} = (5\cdot9;\ 5\cdot4) = (45;\ 20)$

10) $\vec{A} + \vec{B} = (5;\ 7;\ 9)$

11) $|\vec{B}| = \sqrt{2^2 + (-3)^2 + (-4)^2}$
$= \sqrt{4+9+16} = \sqrt{29}$

12) $\vec{A} = (5;\ 4;\ 3),\ \vec{B} = (1;\ 2;\ 3)$
$\vec{C} = 2\vec{A} - 3\vec{B},$
$2\vec{A} = (10;\ 8;\ 6),\ 3\vec{B} = (3;\ 6;\ 9)$
$2\vec{A} - 3\vec{B} = (10-3;\ 8-6;\ 6-9),$
$\vec{C} = (7;\ 2;\ -3)$
$|\vec{C}| = \sqrt{7^2 + 2^2 + (-3)^2} = \sqrt{62}$

13) $\vec{A} + \vec{B} = (6-4;\ 4-2),$
$\vec{A} + \vec{B} = (2;\ 2)$

14) $\vec{A} = (2;\ 2),\ \vec{B} = (3;\ 3),$
$\vec{A} + \vec{B} = (2+3;\ 2+3) = (5;\ 5)$

15) $\vec{A} = (2;\ 4),\ \vec{B} = (2;\ 4),\ \vec{C} = (8;\ -4),$
$\vec{A} + \vec{B} + \vec{C} = (2+2+8;\ 4+4-4) = (12;\ 4)$

TEST– 25
(Solutions)

1) $x^2+y^2=r^2$, $x^2+y^2=7^2 \Rightarrow$ $x^2+y^2=49$

2) $(x–3)^2+(y+6)^2=16$

3) $m(a, b)$, $a=\dfrac{-8}{2}=-4$, $b=\dfrac{-10}{2}=-5$, $m(-4, -5)$

4) $2x^2+2y^2+8x–10y+14=0$
$x^2+y^2+4x–5y+7=0$,
Circle center $(a, b)=\left(\dfrac{-4}{2}, \dfrac{-(-5)}{2}\right)$
$=\left(-2, \dfrac{5}{2}\right)$

5) $(x–2)^2+(y–3)^2=36$

6) Circle center $= (6; 5)$

7) $(x–3)^2+(y–4)^2=5^2$, $r=5$

8) $x^2+y^2=64$

9) $r=\sqrt{(4+2)^2+(-5+9)^2}=\sqrt{36+16}=\sqrt{52}$
$(x–4)^2+(y+5)^2=r^2$,
$(x–4)^2+(y+5)^2=\left(\sqrt{52}\right)^2$,
$(x–4)^2+(y+5)^2=52$

10) $r=\sqrt{(-8-5)^2+(12+2)^2}=$
$=\sqrt{(-13)^2+14^2}=\sqrt{365}$,
$(x+8)^2+(y–12)^2=365$

11) Circle center $= (6; –2)$

12) $(x+3)^2+(y–3)^2=5^2$, $r=5$

13) Circle center $= (a; b) =$
$\left(\dfrac{-16}{2}; \dfrac{24}{2}\right)=(-8; 12)$

14) $x^2+y^2–7x+13y–20=0$
$r=\dfrac{\sqrt{A^2+B^2-4A}}{2}$, $A=–7$, $B=13$, $C=–20$,
$r=\dfrac{\sqrt{(-7)^2+13^2-4(-20)}}{2}=\dfrac{\sqrt{298}}{2}$

15) $x^2+y^2=r^2$,
$x^2+y^2=9^2 \Rightarrow r=9$

TEST– 26
(*Solutions*)

1) $(n–2)\cdot180=540$,
   $n–2=3$, $n=5$

2) $(n–2)\cdot180=1440$,
   $n–2=8$, $n=10$

3) $\alpha=\dfrac{360}{n}=\dfrac{360}{18}=20^{\circ}$
   Interior angle $= 180–20=160^{\circ}$

4) $\alpha=\dfrac{360}{n}=20^{\circ}$, $360=20n$, $n=18$

5) $(n–2)\cdot180=(14–2)\cdot180=12\cdot180=2160^{\circ}$

6) $\angle A+\angle B+\angle C+\angle D+\angle E=360^{\circ}$,
   $60+110+114+20+\angle E=360^{\circ}$, $\angle E=156^{\circ}$,
   $\angle E+\angle x=360^{\circ}$, $156^{\circ}+\angle x=360^{\circ}$, $\angle x=104^{\circ}$

7) $n=\dfrac{360}{6}=60^{\circ}$,
   $n+\alpha=180^{\circ}$, $60^{\circ}+\alpha=180^{\circ}$,
   $\alpha=120^{\circ}$

8) $\alpha=\dfrac{360}{n}=30^{\circ}$,
   $360=30\cdot n$, $n=12$

9) $(n–2)\cdot180=(12–2)\cdot180=1800$

10) $\angle A+\angle B+\angle C+\angle D=360^{\circ}$,
    $110+\alpha+115+90=360^{\circ}$,
    $\alpha=45^{\circ}$

11) $\angle A+\angle B+\angle C+\angle D+\angle E=540^{\circ}$,
    $118+96+x+120+115=540^{\circ}$,
    $x=91^{\circ}$

12) $\alpha=\dfrac{360}{n}=\dfrac{360}{6}=60^{\circ}$

13) $x+\alpha=180^{\circ}$, $x+60^{\circ}=180^{\circ}$,
    $x=120^{\circ}$

14) $A(ABCDEF)=6a=6\cdot10=60$

15) $A(ABCDEF)=6\cdot\left(\dfrac{a^{2}\sqrt{3}}{4}\right)=6\cdot\left(\dfrac{10^{2}\sqrt{3}}{4}\right)=$
    $=6\cdot25\sqrt{3}=150\sqrt{3}\,cm^{2}$

TEST– 27
(*Solutions*)

1) AB=BC,
2x+4=12,
2x=8,
x=4

2) AB=BC,
$x^2-6=30$,
$x^2=36$,
x=6

3) AB=BC,
11=x,
x=11

4) AB=BC,
4x=20,
x=5

5) AB=BC,
3x+6=2x+12,
x=6

6) AB=BC,
$x^2-9=40$,
$x^2=49$,
x=7

7) AD=r=6cm,
$|AB|^2+|AD|^2=|BD|^2$,
$8^2+6^2=|BD|^2$,
$BD^2=100$, BD=10
BC=BD–DC=10–6=4cm

8) AD=DC=r=9cm,
$|AB|^2+|AD|^2=|BD|^2$,
$|AB|^2+9^2=15^2$,
$AB^2=225-81$,
$AB^2=144$,
AB=12

9) $|BC|^2+|2r|^2=|AB|^2$,
$12^2+4r^2=20^2$,
$4r^2=400-144$,
$4r^2=256$,
$r^2=64$,
r=8

10) CK=KD=6cm

11) KM=NL=14cm

12) AB=DC=16cm

13) $|AB|^2+|AO|^2=|BO|^2$,
$12^2+5^2=|BO|^2$,
BO=13cm,
BK=13–5=8cm

14) $|AB|^2+|AO|^2=|BO|^2$,
$24^2+10^2=|BO|^2$,
BO=26cm,
OK=r=10cm,
BK=16, $\dfrac{BK}{OK}=\dfrac{16}{10}=\dfrac{8}{5}$

15) $|AB|^2+|AO|^2=|BO|^2$,
$|AB|^2+4^2=10^2$,
$AB^2=100-16$,
$AB=\sqrt{84}=2\sqrt{21}$

TEST– 28
(*Solutions*)

1) $\overset{\frown}{AB} = \alpha = 80^\circ$

2) $\angle D = \dfrac{\overset{\frown}{ABC}}{2} = 120^\circ$,
$\angle ABC = 240^\circ$

3) $\alpha = x = 66^\circ$

4) $\alpha = \dfrac{\overset{\frown}{ABC}}{2} = \dfrac{220^\circ}{2} = 110^\circ$

5) $70 = \dfrac{x}{2}$, $\Rightarrow x = 140$, $\alpha = \dfrac{140}{2} = 70$,
$x + \angle\alpha = ?, x + \alpha = 140 + 70 = 210$

6) $x = 40$, $y = 36^\circ$,
$2x + 3y = 2 \cdot 40^\circ + 3 \cdot 36^\circ = 80^\circ + 108 = 188^\circ$

7) $\alpha = \dfrac{110 + 70}{2} = \dfrac{180}{2} = 90^\circ$

8) $\overset{\frown}{BCD} = \dfrac{\overset{\frown}{AD} - \overset{\frown}{BD}}{2} = \dfrac{177 - 47}{2} = \dfrac{130}{2} = 65^\circ$

9) $3x = \dfrac{126}{2}$, $3x = 63^\circ$, $x = 21$

10) $\alpha + \angle ADC = 180^\circ$,
$\alpha + 122^\circ = 180^\circ$,
$\alpha = 58^\circ$

11) $\angle C = \dfrac{\overset{\frown}{AE} - \overset{\frown}{BD}}{2} = \dfrac{84 - 24}{2} = \dfrac{60}{2} = 30^\circ$

12) $2x = 60^\circ$, $x = 30^\circ$

13) $\overset{\frown}{AB} = 134^\circ$, $\angle AKC = 88^\circ$, $DC = 2x$
$\dfrac{\overset{\frown}{AB} + \overset{\frown}{DC}}{2} = 92$,
$\dfrac{134 + 2x}{2} = 92$, $134 + 2x = 184$, $x = 25$

14) $\dfrac{\overset{\frown}{AB} + \overset{\frown}{DC}}{2} = 44$, $\dfrac{3x + 2x}{2} = 44$,
$5x = 88$, $x = \dfrac{88}{5}$

15) $\angle A = \dfrac{\overset{\frown}{DE} - \overset{\frown}{BC}}{2} = \dfrac{6x - 2x}{2} = \dfrac{4x}{2} = 2x = 54$
$4x = 54 \cdot 2$, $x = 27$

TEST– 29
(*Solutions*)

1) $6 \cdot 4 = 8 \cdot x$,
$24 = 8x$,
$x = 3$

2) $CB \cdot CA = CD \cdot CE$,
$4 \cdot 14 = 6 \cdot (6+x)$,
$56 = 36 + 6x$,
$6x = 20$, $x = \dfrac{10}{3}$

3) $CB \cdot CA = CD \cdot CE$,
$6 \cdot (6+8) = 7 \cdot (7+x)$,
$6 \cdot 14 = 7 \cdot (7+x)$,
$12 = 7 + x$,
$x = 5$

4) $x^2 = CB \cdot CA$,
$x^2 = 5 \cdot (5+6)$, $\Rightarrow x^2 = 5 \cdot 11$,
$x = \pm\sqrt{55}$

5) $AD \cdot DC = BD \cdot ED$,
$8 \cdot 7 = 3 \cdot x$,
$x = \dfrac{56}{3}$

6) $|AB|^2 = BC \cdot BD$,
$6^2 = 3(3+x)$,
$36 = 3(3+3x)$,
$12 = x + 3$,
$x = 9$

7) $DC \cdot CA = BC \cdot CE$,
$16 \cdot 5 = x \cdot 4x$,
$80 = 4x^2$,
$x^2 = 20$,
$x = 2\sqrt{5}$

8) $12 \cdot 4 = x \cdot 3x$,
$48 = 3x^2$,
$x^2 = 16$,
$x = \pm 4$

9) $2(2+3x) = 2(2+6)$,
$2 + 3x = 2 + 6$,
$3x = 6$,
$x = 2$

10) $6(6+9) = x(x+x)$,
$6 \cdot 15 = x \cdot 2x$,
$45 = x^2$,
$x = 3\sqrt{5}$
Only positive result is answers.

11) $|AB|^2 = BC \cdot BD$,
$8^2 = 4(4+2r)$,
$16 = 4 + 2r$,
$12 = 2r$,
$r = 6$

12) $AB^2 = BC \cdot BD$,
$AB^2 = 4(4+6)$,
$AB = \sqrt{40} = 2\sqrt{10}$

13) $DE \cdot EB = AE \cdot EC$,
$10 \cdot 2 = x \cdot x$,
$x^2 = 20$,
$x = 2\sqrt{5}$

14) $|AB|^2 = 3 \cdot (3+6)$,
$AB^2 = 3 \cdot 9$,
$AB = 3\sqrt{3}$

15) $CB \cdot CA = CD \cdot CE$,
$3 \cdot (3+6) = 2 \cdot (2+x)$,
$27 = 4 + 2x$,
$23 = 2x$,
$x = \dfrac{23}{2}$

TEST– 30
(*Solutions*)

1) $AB = \dfrac{2\pi r\alpha}{360} = \dfrac{2\pi \cdot 6 \cdot 60}{360}$, $AB = 2\pi$

2) $AB = \dfrac{2\pi r\alpha}{360} = \dfrac{2\pi \cdot 3 \cdot 100}{360} = \dfrac{5\pi}{3}$

3) $l = 2\pi r = 2\pi \cdot 5 = 10\pi$

4) $l = 2\pi r = 12\pi$,
   $l = 2\pi r$,
   $2\pi r = 12\pi$,
   $2r = 12$,
   $r = 6$

5) $\overset{\frown}{BC} = \dfrac{2\pi r\alpha}{360} = \dfrac{2\pi \cdot 20 \cdot 30}{360}$,
   $\overset{\frown}{BC} = \dfrac{10\pi}{3}$

6) $l = 2\pi r = 4\sqrt{3}\,\pi$,
   $2r = 4\sqrt{3}$, $r = 2\sqrt{3}$
   $d = 2r = 2 \cdot 2\sqrt{3} = 4\sqrt{3}$

7) $\overset{\frown}{ACD} = \dfrac{2\pi r\alpha}{360} = \dfrac{2\pi \cdot 5 \cdot 140}{360}$,
   $\overset{\frown}{ACD} = \dfrac{35\pi}{9}$

8) $\overset{\frown}{AB} = \dfrac{2\pi r\alpha}{360} = \dfrac{2\pi \cdot 12 \cdot 20}{360}$,
   $\overset{\frown}{AB} = \dfrac{4\pi}{3}$

9) $l = 2\pi r = 2\pi \cdot \sqrt{11}$, $l = 2\pi \sqrt{11}$ cm
   $2r = \sqrt{44}$, $2r = 2\sqrt{11}$, $r = \sqrt{11}$

10) $\overset{\frown}{AB} = 90° = 2y + 20°$, $2y = 70°$, $y = 35°$
    $\angle ABC = 270°$, $270 = 3x + 30$, $3x = 240$, $x = 80°$
    $x + y = 80 + 35 = 115°$

11) $\overset{\frown}{AOB} = \overset{\frown}{AB}$,
    $120° = 3x + 90°$,
    $3x = 30°$,
    $x = 10°$

12) $\text{Area} = \dfrac{\pi r^2 \alpha}{360} = \dfrac{\pi \cdot 16^2 \cdot 120}{360} = \dfrac{256\pi}{3}$

13) $\overset{\frown}{AB} = \dfrac{2\pi r\alpha}{360} = \dfrac{2\pi \cdot \sqrt{3} \cdot 40}{360} = \dfrac{2\pi\sqrt{3}}{9}$

14) $AB = \dfrac{2\pi r\alpha}{360} = \dfrac{2\pi \cdot 18 \cdot 18}{360} = \dfrac{2\pi 18}{20} = \dfrac{9\pi}{5}$

15) $d = 2r = \sqrt{90}$, $2r = 3\sqrt{10}$, $r = \dfrac{3\sqrt{10}}{2}$
    $l = 2\pi r = 2\pi \cdot \dfrac{3\sqrt{10}}{2} = 3\sqrt{10}\pi$

TEST– 31
(*Solutions*)

1) Area=$\pi r^2=\pi\cdot(1,2)^2=1,44\pi$

2) Area=$\pi r^2=196\pi$,
$r^2=196$,
$r=14$

3) Area=$\pi r^2=289\pi$,
$r^2=289$,
$r=17$,
$d=2r=2\cdot17=34$

4) Area $=\dfrac{\pi r^2\alpha}{360}=\dfrac{\pi\cdot6^2\cdot75}{360}=\dfrac{75\pi}{10}=\dfrac{15\pi}{2}$

5) Area $=\dfrac{\pi r^2\alpha}{360}=\dfrac{\pi\cdot18^2\cdot110}{360}=99\pi$

6) Area $=\dfrac{\pi r^2\alpha}{360}=\dfrac{\pi\cdot12^2\cdot140}{360}=56\pi$

7) $AB=2r=4\sqrt{3},\ r=2\sqrt{3}$,
Area= $\pi r^2=\pi\left(2\sqrt{3}\right)^2=12\pi$

8) Area(AOB) $=\dfrac{\pi r^2\alpha}{360}=\dfrac{\pi\cdot6^2\cdot60}{360}=6\pi$
Area $\triangle AOB=\dfrac{r^2\sqrt{3}}{4}=\dfrac{6^2\cdot\sqrt{3}}{4}=9\sqrt{3}$
Shaded region $=6\pi-9\sqrt{3}$

9) Area $=\dfrac{\pi r^2\alpha}{360}=\dfrac{\pi\cdot6^2\cdot330}{360}=33\pi$

10) $AO=12=R=6,\ $ Area(1)$=\pi r^2=36\pi$,
$BC=6=R=3,\ $ Area(2)$=\pi r^2=9\pi$,
Shaded region $=36\pi-9\pi=27\pi$

11) Area(ABCDEF) $=\dfrac{6a^2\sqrt{3}}{4}$
$=\dfrac{6\cdot36\cdot\sqrt{3}}{4}=54\sqrt{3}$
Area Circle $=\pi r^2=\pi\left(3\sqrt{3}\right)^2=27\pi\,\mathrm{cm}^2$
Shaded Re g ion $=\dfrac{54\sqrt{3}-27\pi}{6}$
$=\dfrac{18\sqrt{3}-9\pi}{2}$

12) Area $=\dfrac{\pi r^2\alpha}{360}=\dfrac{\pi\cdot4^2\cdot108}{360}=\dfrac{24\pi}{5}$

13) $\dfrac{A_1}{A_2}=\dfrac{\pi r_1^2}{\pi r_2^2}=\dfrac{\left(4\sqrt{3}\right)^2}{\left(4\sqrt{2}\right)^2}=\dfrac{3}{2}$

14) Area $=\dfrac{\pi r^2}{2}=\dfrac{\pi\cdot\left(\sqrt{11}\right)^2}{2}=\dfrac{11\pi}{2}$

15) Area(1) $=\pi r^2=\pi\cdot4^2=16\pi$,
Area(2) $=\pi r^2=\pi\cdot2^2=4\pi$,
Shaded Area $=16\pi-4\pi=12\pi$

TEST– 32
(*Solutions*)

1) a=12, b=7, c=8,
Area=2(ab+ac+bc)=2·(12·7+12·8+7·8)=
$\qquad$ =2· (98+96+56)=500

2) a=6, b=4, c=3,
Area=2·(ab+ac+bc)=2·(6·4+6·3+4·3)=
$\qquad$ =2· (24+18+12)=108

3) a=10, b=8, c=6,
Area=2·(ab+ac+bc)=2·(8·10+10·6+6·8)=
$\qquad$ =2· (80+60+48)=196

4) Area: 2·(ab+ac+bc)
a=3, b=4, c=5,
Area=2·(3·4+3·5+4·5)=2· (12+15+20)=94

5) A=2·(a²+ab+ab)=2a²+4a·h=
$\qquad$ =2·8²+4·8·3=128+96=224

6) a=4, b=6, c=7,
Area=2·(ab+ac+bc)=2·(4·6+4·7+6·7)=
$\qquad$ =2·(24+28+42)=188

7) |FD|²+|FC|²=|DC|², 12²+9²=|DC|²,
DC=15, DC=AB=15, h=13cm.
Base Perimeter=(9+12+15)=36cm
Aside=h·Perimeter=13·36=468
Abase=2·$\left(\dfrac{9 \cdot 12}{2}\right)$=108
A=468+108=576

8) |AF|²+|FB|²=|AB|², 5²+12²=|AB|², AB=13,
Aside=Base · Perimeter · x height=
$\qquad$ =(5+12+13)·8=240cm²

9) $\dfrac{1}{a}+\dfrac{1}{b}+\dfrac{1}{c}=3$, $\dfrac{bc+ac+ab}{abc}=3$,
(bc+ac+ab)=3·abc, (ab+ac+bc)=3·144=432,
A=2·(ab+ac+bc)=2·432=864.

10) S=2πr²+2πrh=2π·4²+2π·4·5
$\qquad$ =32π+40π=72πcm²

11) S=2πr²+2πrh=2π·3²+2π·3·6
$\qquad$ =18π+36π=54πcm²

12) S=2πr²+2πrh=2π·6²+2π·6·11
$\qquad$ =72π+132π=204π

13) S=2πr²+2πrh=2π·(3x)²+2π·3x·2x=
$\qquad$ =2π·9x²+12π·x²=18π·x²+12π·x²=30πx²

14) $\dfrac{r}{h}=\dfrac{1}{3} \Rightarrow h=3r$,
S=2πr²+2πrh=2π·r²+2π·r·3r
$\qquad$ =2π·r²+6π·r²=8πr²

15) AB=2r=3²ˣ, $r=\dfrac{3^{2x}}{2} \Rightarrow h=3^x$,
S=2πr²+2πrh=2π·$\left(\dfrac{3^{2x}}{2}\right)^2$+2π·$\dfrac{3^{2x}}{2}$·3ˣ=
=2π·$\dfrac{3^{4x}}{4}$+π·3³ˣ=$\dfrac{3^{4x} \pi}{2}$+3³ˣ·π

TEST– 33
(*Solutions*)

1) Solution= B+L=16+3·9=16+27=43

2) Base area = $a^2=12^2=144cm^2$

3) Base area = $a^2=225$,
   a=15cm

4) Base area = $a^2=16^2=256cm^2$

5) AK=6, CM=CD=$\frac{16}{2}=8$,

   AM=$\sqrt{6^2+8^2}=10cm$

   S Side=4·$\left(\frac{16\cdot10}{2}\right)=2\cdot160=320$,

   All area=256+320=576

6) The base is square. The area is S^2. So the
   base is 6^2 or $36cm^2$.

   S=B+$\frac{1}{2}$P·L ,

   S=36+$\frac{1}{2}$(8·6)·4

   S=36+96=132cm^2

7) The base is square. The area is base S^2.
   Base area=4^2=16

   S=B+$\frac{1}{2}$P·L =16+$\frac{1}{2}$·(4·5·4) = 56

8) Base area = $a^2=9^2=81$,

   S=B+$\frac{1}{2}$B·L ,

   S=81+$\frac{1}{2}$(4·9·12) = 297

9) With a radius of 4cm and slant height of
   8cm given.
   S=$\pi r^2+\pi rl=\pi\cdot4^2+\pi\cdot4\cdot8=16\pi+32\pi=48\pi$.

10) S=$\pi r^2+\pi rl=\pi\cdot5^2+\pi\cdot5\cdot13=25\pi+65\pi=90\pi$.

11) S=$\pi r^2+\pi rl=\pi\cdot6^2+\pi\cdot6\cdot16=36\pi+96\pi=132\pi$.

12) $|CK|^2+|KB|^2=|CB|^2$,
    $5^2+12^2=|CB|^2$,
    CB=13

13) $|AK|^2+|KC|^2=|AC|^2$, AC=l=25cm.
    S=$\pi r^2+\pi rl=\pi\cdot12^2+\pi\cdot12\cdot20$
    $=144\pi+240\pi=384\pi$.

14) S=$\pi r^2+\pi rl=\pi\cdot4^2+\pi\cdot4\cdot2\sqrt{13}=16\pi+8\sqrt{13}\ \pi$.

15) $|AD|^2+|DC|^2=|AC|^2$,
    $12^2+10^2=|AC|^2$,
    AC=$2\sqrt{61}$.

TEST– 34
(*Solutions*)

1) $V=a^3=6^3=216cm^3$

2) $V=a\cdot b\cdot c=10\cdot 6\cdot 8,$
    $V=480cm^3$

3) $V=a\cdot b\cdot c,\ 240=4\cdot x\cdot 5,$
    $x=6cm$

4) Volume=Area x length=36x13=468cm^3

5) $V=a\cdot b\cdot c,\ V=x\cdot 2x\cdot 4x=64,$
    $8x^3=64,\ x^3=8,\ x=2cm$
    $2x=2\cdot 2=4$

6) $V=a^3,\ V=7^3,\ V=343$

7) $V=a\cdot b\cdot c,\ V=5\cdot 6\cdot 14=420cm^3$

8) $\dfrac{V_1}{V_2}=\dfrac{a^3}{a\cdot b\cdot c}=\dfrac{6^3}{10\cdot 6\cdot 8},\ \dfrac{V_1}{V_2}=\dfrac{9}{20}$

9) $V=\pi\cdot r^2\cdot h=\pi\cdot 4^2\cdot 8=\pi\cdot 16\cdot 8=128\pi$

10) $V=\pi\cdot r^2\cdot h=\pi\cdot 4^2\cdot 4=64\pi$

11) $V=\pi\cdot r^2\cdot h,\ V=\pi\cdot 2^2\cdot 12,\ V=\pi\cdot 4\cdot 12,\ V=48\pi$

12) $V=\pi\cdot r^2\cdot h=\pi\cdot 6^2\cdot 10=360\pi$

13) $V=\pi\cdot r^2\cdot h=\pi\cdot 3^2\cdot 14=\pi\cdot 9\cdot 14=126\pi$

14) $V=\pi\cdot r^2\cdot h=\pi\cdot 8^2\cdot 18=\pi\cdot 64\cdot 18=1152\pi$

15) $V_1=\pi\cdot r^2\cdot h=\pi\cdot 10^2\cdot 12=1200\pi$
    $V_2=\pi\cdot r^2\cdot h=\pi\cdot 6^2\cdot 10=360\pi$
    $\dfrac{V_1}{V_2}=\dfrac{1200\pi}{360\pi}=\dfrac{10}{3}$

TEST– 35
(*Solutions*)

1) Area of square = $S^2=a^2=12^2=144$cm^2,
Height=20cm,
$V=\dfrac{1}{3}$B·h$=\dfrac{1}{3}\cdot144\cdot20=48\cdot20=960$cm^3

2) Base area$=a^2=14^2=196$cm^2, Height=20cm,
$V=\dfrac{1}{3}$B·h$=\dfrac{1}{3}\cdot196\cdot16=1045$cm^3

3) Base area$=\dfrac{9\cdot12}{2}=54$cm^2,
$V=\dfrac{1}{3}$B·h$=\dfrac{1}{3}\cdot16\cdot54=288$cm^3

4) Base area$=\dfrac{a^2\cdot\sqrt{3}}{4}=\dfrac{6^2\cdot\sqrt{3}}{4}$
$=\dfrac{36\sqrt{3}}{4}=9\sqrt{3}$ cm^2,
$V=\dfrac{1}{3}$B·h$=\dfrac{9\sqrt{3}\cdot8}{3}=24\sqrt{3}$ cm^3

5) Base area$=a^2=12^2=144$cm^2,
$V=\dfrac{1}{3}$B·h$=\dfrac{1}{3}\cdot144\cdot14=48\cdot14=672$cm^3

6) Base area$=6\cdot\dfrac{a^2\cdot\sqrt{3}}{4}$
$=6\cdot\dfrac{10^2\cdot\sqrt{3}}{4}=150\sqrt{3}$ cm^2,
$V=\dfrac{1}{3}$B·h$=\dfrac{1}{3}\cdot150\sqrt{3}\cdot18=900\sqrt{3}$ cm^3

7) Base area$=\dfrac{a^2\cdot\sqrt{3}}{4}$
$=\dfrac{15^2\cdot\sqrt{3}}{4}=\dfrac{225\sqrt{3}}{4}$ cm^2,
$V=\dfrac{B\cdot h}{3}=\dfrac{225\sqrt{3}}{4}\cdot\dfrac{21}{3}$
$=\dfrac{1575\sqrt{3}}{4}=394\sqrt{3}$ cm^3

8) Base area$=a^2=20^2=400$cm^2,
$V=\dfrac{1}{3}$B·h$=\dfrac{400\cdot22}{3}=\dfrac{8800}{3}$ cm^3

9) $V=\dfrac{1}{3}$B·h$=\dfrac{1}{3}\pi r^2\cdot h=\dfrac{1}{3}\pi\cdot6^2\cdot10=120\pi$

10) Base area$=\pi r^2=\pi\cdot5^2=25\pi$,
$V=\dfrac{1}{3}$B·h$=\dfrac{1}{3}25\pi\cdot8=\dfrac{200\pi}{3}$

11) Base$=\pi r^2=\pi \cdot 7^2=49\pi$,

$$V=\frac{1}{3}B \cdot h = \frac{49\pi \cdot 10}{3} = \frac{490\pi}{3}$$

12) $V=\frac{1}{3}\pi r^2 \cdot h$, $\quad \frac{1}{3}\pi \cdot 6^2 h = 120\pi$,

$\pi \cdot 36h=360\pi$, h=10cm.

13) $V=\frac{1}{3}\pi r^2 \cdot h$, $\quad \frac{1}{3}\pi \cdot r^2 h = 128\pi$,

$\pi \cdot r^2 8=3 \cdot 128\pi$, $r^2=3 \cdot 16$, $r=4\sqrt{3}$ cm.

14) $V=\frac{B \cdot h}{3} = \frac{\pi r^2 \cdot h}{3}$,

$$V=\frac{\pi(2x)^2 \cdot 3x}{3} = \frac{\pi 4x^2 3x}{3} = \pi 4x^3$$

15) $V=\frac{1}{3}B \cdot h = \frac{1}{3}\pi r^2 \cdot h$

$$=\frac{1}{3}\pi \cdot \left(\sqrt{5}\right)^2 \cdot \sqrt{7} = \frac{5\pi\sqrt{7}}{3}$$

TEST– 36
(*Solutions*)

1) $S=4\pi r^2=4\pi\ (11)^2=4\cdot121\pi=484\pi$

2) $S=4\pi r^2=4\pi(13)^2=4\cdot169\pi=676\pi$

3) $S=4\pi r^2=4\pi(12,2)^2=4\cdot148,84\pi=595,36\pi$

4) $S=4\pi r^2=4\pi(7)^2=4\cdot49\pi=196\pi$

5) $S=4\pi r^2=4\pi(6,3)^2=4\cdot39,69\pi=158,76\pi$

6) $S=4\pi r^2,$
$400\pi=4\cdot\pi r^2,$
$100=r^2,$
$r=10$

7) $S=4\pi r^2,$
$S=4\pi(3\pi)^2=4\pi\cdot9\pi^2=36\pi^2$

8) $V=\dfrac{4}{3}\pi r^3=\dfrac{4}{3}\pi\cdot4^3=\dfrac{4\cdot64\pi}{3},$
$V=268cm^3$

9) $V=\dfrac{4}{3}\pi r^3=\dfrac{4}{3}\pi(3,3)^3=\dfrac{4}{3}\pi\cdot36=12\pi=37,7$

10) $V=\dfrac{4}{3}\pi r^3=\dfrac{4}{3}\pi(10)^3=\dfrac{4\pi\cdot1000}{3}=4287\,cm^3$

11) $V=\dfrac{4}{3}\pi r^3,\ 200\pi=\dfrac{4}{3}\pi r^3,$
$200\cdot3=4\pi r^3,\ 50\cdot3=r^3,\ r^3=150,\ r=5\sqrt{2}\ cm$

12) $V=\dfrac{4}{3}\pi r^3=\dfrac{4}{3}\pi(2\pi)^3=\dfrac{4}{3}\pi\cdot8\pi^3=\dfrac{32\pi^4}{3}$

13) $\dfrac{V_1}{V_2}=\dfrac{\dfrac{4}{3}\pi r_1^3}{\dfrac{4}{3}\pi r_2^3}=\dfrac{r_1^3}{r_2^3}=\dfrac{3^3}{2^3}=\dfrac{27}{8}$

14) $V=\dfrac{4}{3}\pi r^3=\dfrac{4}{3}\pi(2,2)^3=\dfrac{4}{3}\pi\cdot10,648=44,6$

15) $V=\dfrac{4}{3}\pi r^3,$
$160\pi=\dfrac{4}{3}\pi r^3,$
$160\cdot3=4r^3,$
$120=r^3,$
$r=2\sqrt[3]{15}$

TEST– 37
(*Solutions*)

1) $A+B=\begin{bmatrix} 8 & 8 \\ 5 & 7 \end{bmatrix}$

2) $A-B=\begin{bmatrix} 3 & 7 \\ 4 & 1 \end{bmatrix}$

3) $3A=3\cdot\begin{bmatrix} 4 & 3 \\ 2 & 7 \end{bmatrix}=\begin{bmatrix} 12 & 9 \\ 6 & 21 \end{bmatrix}$

4) $3A=3\cdot\begin{bmatrix} 6 & 4 \\ 3 & 2 \end{bmatrix}=\begin{bmatrix} 18 & 12 \\ 9 & 6 \end{bmatrix}$

$2B=2\cdot\begin{bmatrix} 2 & 3 \\ 1 & 2 \end{bmatrix}=\begin{bmatrix} 4 & 6 \\ 1 & 4 \end{bmatrix}$

$3A-2B=\begin{bmatrix} 14 & 12 \\ 8 & 2 \end{bmatrix}$

5) $14=2x,\ x=7,$
$16=4y,\ y=4,$
$x+y=11$

6) $10=5x,\ x=2,$
$14=7y,\ y=2,$
$2x+3y=10$

7) $A+B=\begin{bmatrix} 4 & 4 \\ 5 & 5 \end{bmatrix}$

8) $A\cdot B=\begin{bmatrix} 2 & 6 \\ 4 & 18 \end{bmatrix}$

9) $2A=2\cdot\begin{bmatrix} 1 & 2 & 3 \\ 4 & 6 & 7 \end{bmatrix}=\begin{bmatrix} 2 & 4 & 6 \\ 8 & 12 & 14 \end{bmatrix}$

10) $\begin{bmatrix} 7 & 2 \\ 5 & -10 \\ 25 & 9 \end{bmatrix}$

11) $\begin{bmatrix} 1 & 8 \\ 2 & 9 \\ 4 & 10 \end{bmatrix}$

12) $\begin{bmatrix} 2 & 8 & 11 \\ 4 & 9 & 12 \\ 6 & 10 & 3 \end{bmatrix}$

13) $A=\begin{bmatrix} 1 & 2 \\ 3 & 4 \end{bmatrix},\ B^{T}=\begin{bmatrix} 5 & 7 \\ 6 & 8 \end{bmatrix},$

$A+B^{T}=\begin{bmatrix} 6 & 9 \\ 9 & 12 \end{bmatrix}$

14) $3A=\begin{bmatrix} 3 & 6 & 9 \\ -6 & 9 & 12 \end{bmatrix},\ 2B=\begin{bmatrix} -4 & 8 & 6 \\ 4 & 0 & 2 \end{bmatrix}$

$3A+2B=\begin{bmatrix} -1 & 14 & 15 \\ -2 & 9 & 14 \end{bmatrix}$

15) $A^{T}=\begin{bmatrix} 1 & 3 \\ 2 & 4 \end{bmatrix},\ 2A^{T}=\begin{bmatrix} 2 & 6 \\ 4 & 8 \end{bmatrix},$

$B^{T}=\begin{bmatrix} 5 & 7 \\ 6 & 8 \end{bmatrix},\ 3B^{T}=\begin{bmatrix} 15 & 21 \\ 18 & 24 \end{bmatrix},$

$2A^{T}+3B^{T}=\begin{bmatrix} 17 & 27 \\ 22 & 32 \end{bmatrix}$

555 Geometry - Test Answers

Test No	Q1	Q2	Q3	Q4	Q5	Q6	Q7	Q8	Q9	Q10	Q11	Q12	Q13	Q14	Q15
Test-1	C	D	B	C	A	A	E	A	D	D	B	A	A	C	E
Test-2	C	C	E	D	E	D	B	C	A	C	B	D	E	C	D
Test-3	E	A	E	B	E	C	7	C	B	E	B	E	E	A	C
Test-4	B	E	A	C	E	D	E	C	E	E	E	E	A	B	C
Test-5	B	C	D	D	E	B	B	A	A	D	D	C	B	E	E
Test-6	C	B	E	E	A	C	A	D	C	A	C	A	D	B	E
Test-7	B	A	C	E	E	B	E	B	A	E	C	E	C	C	D
Test-8	B	A	D	D	B	D	D	E	B	E	E	E	E	A	E
Test-9	E	B	E	A	D	A	B	D	A	E	B	D	A	D	A
Test-10	B	C	A	A	A	D	E	E	B	D	D	C	C	C	E
Test-11	A	C	A	D	D	E	B	A	C	D	A	A	C	C	D
Test-12	B	A	E	E	B	E	A	D	D	C	C	E	C	E	B
Test-13	E	B	C	A	E	A	D	C	B	D	C	A	C	A	D
Test-14	C	A	C	D	E	C	D	A	C	A	E	D	D	A	D
Test-15	E	E	C	B	C	B	A	D	B	A	A	C	C	B	C
Test-16	C	A	C	E	C	D	B	C	B	B	E	E	D	B	C
Test-17	C	E	B	E	D	A	D	C	D	B	A	A	D	C	D
Test-18	D	D	C	D	B	E	E	A	A	B	B	A	C	D	C
Test-19	A	B	C	C	E	B	D	C	D	E	A	C	A	E	D
Test-20	A	A	C	B	A	B	D	A	E	C	B	A	A	E	D
Test-21	E	C	D	D	A	E	E	A	E	D	A	E	E	A	D
Test-22	C	C	E	A	E	E	D	E	C	E	B	C	E	A	D
Test-23	B	E	A	E	C	A	E	A	E	A	D	D	E	C	A
Test-24	A	C	E	E	C	E	C	D	E	A	B	D	C	E	E
Test-25	C	D	C	B	B	C	C	A	B	E	E	D	D	D	C
Test-26	D	C	B	B	D	E	E	C	D	A	A	D	C	E	C
Test-27	E	C	E	B	E	B	D	C	A	E	E	A	C	E	A
Test-28	A	D	D	E	B	B	C	B	A	B	C	D	B	D	E
Test-29	C	E	E	C	B	D	C	C	B	D	D	B	D	E	B
Test-30	B	D	E	E	A	D	E	C	E	E	B	D	A	C	A
Test-31	C	D	C	E	A	E	A	C	C	A	E	D	D	A	A
Test-32	E	D	A	B	E	D	A	C	E	D	A	C	B	C	B
Test-33	A	B	D	D	C	E	E	C	A	C	A	D	B	A	B
Test-34	D	B	A	B	A	E	E	B	C	A	B	D	E	B	A
Test-35	B	C	D	E	A	D	C	B	B	B	E	A	C	D	E
Test-36	E	E	B	B	A	E	C	A	A	C	B	D	A	C	B
Test-37	A	B	D	C	A	A	B	C	B	B	A	D	C	A	B

About the Author

Tayyip Oral, M.Ed & MBA

Tayyip Oral is a mathematician and test prep expert who has been teaching in learning centers and high school test since 1998. Mr. Oral is the founder of 555 math book series which includes variety of mathematics books. Tayyip Oral graduated from Qafqaz university with a Bachelor`s degree in Industrial Engineering. He later received his Master`s degree in Business Administration from the same university. He is an educator who has written several SAT Math, ACT Math, Geometry, Math counts and Math IQ books. He lives in Houston,TX.

Books by Tayyip Oral

1. Tayyip Oral, Dr. Steve Warner. 555 Math IQ Questions for Middle School Students: Improve Your Critical Thinking with 555 Questions and Answer, 2015

2. Tayyip Oral, Dr. Steve Warner, Serife Oral, Algebra Handbook for Gifted Middle School Students, 2015

3. Tayyip Oral, Geometry Formula Handbook, 2015

4. Tayyip Oral, IQ Intelligence Questions for Middle and High School Students, 2014

5. Tayyip Oral, Dr. Steve Warner, Serife Oral, 555 Geometry Problems for High School Students: 135 Questions with Solutions, 2015

6. Tayyip Oral, Sevket Oral, 555 Math IQ questions for Elementary School Student, 2015

7. Tayyip Oral, 555 ACT Math, 555 Questions with Solutions, 2015

8. Tayyip Oral, Sevket Oral, 555 ACT Math - II, 555 Questions with Answers, 2016

9. Tayyip Oral, 555 Geometry (555 Questions with Solutions), 2016

10. Tayyip Oral, Dr. Steve Warner, 555 Advanced math problems, 2015

11. T. Oral, E. Seyidzade, Araz publishing, Master's Degree Program Preparation (IQ), Cag Ogretim, Araz Courses, Baku, Azerbaijan, 2010.
    A master's degree program preparation text book for undergraduate students in Azerbaijan.

12. T. Oral, M. Aranli, F. Sadigov and N. Resullu, Resullu Publishing, Baku, Azerbaijan - 2012 (3.edition)
    A text book for job placement exam in Azerbaijan for undergraduate and post undergraduate students in Azerbaijan.

13. T. Oral and I. Hesenov, Algebra (Text book), Nurlar Printing and Publishing, Baku, Azerbaijan, 2001.
    A text book covering algebra concepts and questions with detailed explanations at high school level in Azerbaijan.

14. T.Oral, I.Hesenov, S.Maharramov, and J.Mikaylov, Geometry (Text book), Nurlar Printing and Publishing, Baku, Azerbaijan, 2002.
    A text book for high school students to prepare them for undergraduate education in Azerbaijan.

15. T. Oral, I. Hesenov, and S. Maharramov, Geometry Formulas (Text Book), Araz courses, Baku, Azerbaijan, 2003.
    A text book for high school students' university exam preparation in Azerbaijan.

16. T. Oral, I. Hesenov, and S. Maharramov, Algebra Formulas (Text Book), Araz courses, Baku, Azerbaijan, 2000
    A university exam preparation text book for high school students in Azerbaijan.

Made in the USA
Columbia, SC
28 June 2024

37696165R00072